How often have you cri~~~~~~~~~~~~~~~~ can leave her two-year-o~~ with you for the morning, winced when the garage mechanic tells you that your car's repairs are going to cost twice what he'd estimated, wilted when a man got the promotion that should have been yours—but been too afraid to do anything about it?

Well—
NOW IS THE TIME TO START TO:

Know how you feel
Say what you mean
Get what you want

Assertive training techniques will help you to shake off the shackles of self-defeating behavior once and for all by showing you

- how to recognize your assertion problems
- simple ways to get rid of anxiety
- how to build your own assertive skills
- how to combat irrational beliefs
- how to deal openly and effectively with sex problems, business hassles, family squabbles, doctors, storekeepers, mechanics, salespeople, in-laws, lovers and more!

Whether you just want to say *no* to your boss or *yes* to your goals, this practical, complete guide to assertive training will tell you everything you need to know to start standing up for you today!

The New Assertive Woman

Lynn Z. Bloom, Karen Coburn
and Joan Pearlman

Published by
Dell Publishing Co., Inc.
1 Dag Hammarskjold Plaza
New York, New York 10017

Chart in Chapter 9 used by permission of Margaret C. Fagin.
Copyright © 1975 by Lynn Z. Bloom, Karen Levin Coburn
and Joan Crystal Pearlman

Laurel ® TM 674623, Dell Publishing Co., Inc.

ISBN: 0-440-36393-4

Reprinted by arrangement with Delacorte Press

Printed in the United States of America

October 1980
10 9

WFH

Acknowledgments

We wish to acknowledge our adaptation of the theories of the following: Joseph Wolpe, Arnold Lazarus, and Patricia Jakubowski-Spector, behavior modification; Eric Berne, transactional analysis; Allen Ivey and Robert Carkhuff, techniques of skillful listening; Albert Ellis, rational emotive therapy.

We would like particularly to express our appreciation to all the women in the assertive training groups we have worked with; from them we have learned and grown. To maintain the confidentiality of our group members, where we have drawn examples from real life we have altered the particulars to avoid personal identification.

Thanks to our husbands, Martin Bloom, Stephen Coburn, and Alan Pearlman, for their understanding and cooperation during the writing of this book. We also thank our children, Bard and Laird Bloom, Andrew and Alison Coburn, Chee, Karen, and Marnae Pearlman. In being themselves they have given us additional insights into our subject—as well as some respite from it.

For their help and suggestions we would like to thank: Jane Anton, Maria Ballesteros, Linda Barton, Martin Bloom, Joan Cohen, Patt Denning, Margaret Fagin, Ann Fitzgerald, Peggy Guest, Ramona Howard, Beverly Hotchner, Lyn Jenkins, Mary Kirkpatrick, Sue Lewis, Cheri May, Anna Navarro, Diana Richards, Mary Ellen Schwartz, Linda Skrainka, Abby Snay, Susan Spieldoch, Madge Treeger, and our sisters at the St. Louis Women's Counseling Center.

We are grateful, too, for the assistance of Betty Kelly,

5

Delacorte Senior Editor, whose intelligence and talent have contributed greatly to this book.

St. Louis, Mo.
May, 1975

Lynn Z. Bloom
Karen Levin Coburn
Joan Crystal Pearlman

To the New Assertive Woman everywhere—
in practice, in process, in promise.

Contents

Introduction

Why should assertiveness be such a problem for women?

No matter how "liberated" or successful women are becoming, there are recesses in all our lives where we find ourselves still hesitant to claim our rights, still anxious about our feelings, unable to respond to anger, and, above all, frustrated by the powerlessness we endure in our relations with doctors, lawyers, hairdressers, colleagues, and our families. We avoid conflict, in the words of the authors of this book. We subordinate our wishes to those of others, and by being non-assertive, we are natural victims for every aggressor.

We always knew this was true, that there was a kind of disability in our femininity. Long ago Margaret Mead said women are "unsexed by success," and we did feel guilty and fearful when we won. But until the new feminism stimulated research into sex-role socialization, we did not know what to name our disabilities or how to deal with them. Now we have some theory. There is the "fear of success" syndrome that psychologist Matina Horner documented in her now famous study of bright college women yearning to do well in school, but frightened that their very suc-

11

cess would make them deviant. There is the theory of the double bind in all its variations: "You are too pretty to be competent," "You are too tough to have around." There are the humiliations young women endure at the hands of men and other women, according to psychologist Martha Kent, who is studying the training and professional experiences of academic women. And there are the stultifying limits imposed by the cherished notion that male and female roles are opposite and non-overlapping. Thus, we are other-directed and oversensitive to other people's expectations of us, because the line between passivity and aggressiveness (or between any other traditionally male/female characteristic, for that matter) is not clearly defined at all. Rather, deviance is always just one degree beyond what he (or they) will tolerate in a woman.

The New Assertive Woman is not simply a description of a new kind of female behavior. It is a how-to manual aimed at curing passivity and powerlessness in interpersonal relations. Philosophically it rests on a stirring call for a "bill of personal rights" which will transform women's deepest sense of self and personal environment. Drawing upon reports of dozens of "assertive training groups," *The New Assertive Woman* teaches one to recognize interpersonal entrapment and provides a series of exercises designed to change one's situation.

Surely the right to be treated with respect, to have and to express feelings, opinions, and wants, to be listened to and taken seriously by other persons, to set one's own priorities, to say *no* without feeling guilty, and to get what one pays for are fundamental rights of human beings. It is amazing but nonetheless necessary that a book had to be written to tell women that they have such rights and to teach them how to ask for them.

—SHEILA TOBIAS
Associate Provost
Wesleyan University
April 1975

1

Assertive Training and Why It Is So Important for Women

THE *beds are made and the breakfast dishes are done. You've taken out the trash, watered the plants, and fed the dog. All is quiet. Now, finally, you have some time for yourself—to do what you want to do. Two hours just for yourself.*

The phone rings. It's a close friend asking if you would please, as a very special favor, watch Alison (her two-year-old) for the morning while she goes to a meeting. You have a familiar sinking feeling in your stomach. You really wanted this time to yourself.

What would you do? And, even more important, what mix of attitudes and ideas affects your choice about what to do, and about how you feel about yourself and others?

That's what this book, *The New Assertive Woman*, is all about. It presents information to help us pinpoint what our real feelings are, and techniques to help us communicate directly, honestly, and appropriately. We can do this without infringing on the rights of others, and we can feel comfortable with our own new behavior. This is what being *assertive* is all about.

The Nature of Assertiveness

Assertive behavior is, as we see it, the "golden mean" between *aggressiveness*, at one extreme, and *non-assertiveness*, at the other. "Assertive" is never to be confused with "aggressive." The intent of assertive behavior is to *communicate honestly and directly*. The intent of aggressive behavior is to *dominate*, to get your own way at the expense of others. The intent of non-assertive behavior is to *avoid conflict* altogether, which usually means that you have to *subordinate* your wishes to those of others. When we are aggressive we are insensitive to others' rights, and we express ourselves in ways that demean, humiliate, or coerce them. When we are non-assertive we are natural victims for the aggressor. We either don't tell others what we want and think, or we try to get what we want through devious means. We let others choose for us and infringe on our rights. When we are assertive we make choices for ourselves without harming or being harmed by others.

The distinctions between "aggressive," "assertive," and "non-assertive" ways of behaving may be shown clearly by looking at the different ways you could have reacted to your friend's request for babysitting—assuming, that is, that you didn't want to do it. If you were *aggressive* you could have said, "You're always asking me to do favors for you and you never do anything for me! And besides, Alison always makes a terrible mess in my house. No thanks—I won't do it!"

If you were *non-assertive* you could simply deny your own wishes, and agree to care for Alison: "Well, I was going to do something else, but it really doesn't matter. O.K., bring her over."

Or you could say, *assertively,* "I know it's a drag to take Alison with you, but I've set aside two hours for myself this morning, so I won't be able to take her today."

What determines how you will answer? The experiences of a lifetime, the pressures of our culture, and the preconceived notions about the roles women are supposed to play. Many of us would probably give in and care for Alison whether we wanted to or not.

If you had wanted to babysit for Alison and chose to say *yes,* then there would be no problem for you in your relationship with your friend. But if you had agreed to babysit because you were afraid to say *no,* or didn't know how to refuse without coming on too strong, and if this sort of thing happens to you fairly often, then assertive training just might help you make dramatic changes for the better.

Comparing Non-Assertive, Aggressive, and Assertive Behavior and their Consequences

---

Non-Assertive Behavior

Characteristics of non-assertive behavior include not expressing your own feelings, needs, and ideas; ignoring your own rights; and allowing others to infringe on them. This behavior is usually emotionally dishonest, indirect, inhibited, and self-denying. The non-assertive woman allows others to choose for her and often ends up feeling anxious and disappointed with herself at the time and possibly angry and resentful later.

Why does she do this? She hopes to avoid unpleasant and risky situations, to steer clear of confrontation, tension, and conflict. The problem with this non-assertive behavior is that she usually doesn't get what she needs, her anger builds up, and she doesn't feel good about herself.

Aggressive Behavior

Characteristics of aggressive behavior include expressing your feelings, needs, and ideas at the expense of others; standing up for your own rights but ignoring the rights of others, trying to *dominate*, even *humiliate* them. True, this behavior is expressive, but it is usually defensive, hostile, and self-defeating. The aggressive woman tries to make choices for herself and for others and she usually ends up feeling angry, self-righteous, and possibly guilty later.

Why does she do this? It is a way of venting her anger, and sometimes she achieves her goals, as least in the short run. The problem is, though, that she distances herself from other people and can end up feeling frustrated, bitter, and alone.

Assertive Behavior

Characteristics of assertive behavior include expressing your feelings, needs, and ideas and standing up for your legitimate rights in ways that don't violate the rights of others. This behavior is usually emotionally honest, direct, expressive, and self-enhancing. The assertive woman makes her own choices, is usually confident, and feels good about herself, both while she is being assertive and later.

What's in it for her? She usually achieves her goals, and even when she doesn't she still feels good about herself, knowing that she has been straightforward.

Acting assertively reinforces her good feelings about herself, improves her self-confidence, and leads to freer, more honest relationships with others.

What Is Assertive Training?

Assertive training is based on the theory that our social behavior is learned and so can be unlearned and replaced by new, more rewarding behavior. Once we have tried out some new ways of acting and gotten positive results, we are likely to continue behaving in these new ways.

What assertive training is trying to do is help people shake off their self-defeating non-assertive or aggressive ways in favor of healthier assertive ones, and develop self-esteem along the way. The process teaches us to tell the difference between non-assertive, assertive, and aggressive behavior, and to figure out which situations are apt to give each of us the most trouble with our own assertiveness. Then it teaches us to begin to flex our assertive muscles, gradually at first, in low-risk situations, until before long we are beginning to express our feelings and needs in straightforward ways and, we are beginning to feel good about it. In short, assertive training helps women start to take responsibility for their own lives.

This is not to say that every time a woman asserts herself she gets what she wants. It is never that simple, and there are always some risks involved. But at least the assertive woman has made her own choice rather than allowing someone else to choose for her (or insisting on choosing for others). The fact that she has come right out and said what she is feeling is likely to make her feel good about herself, to increase her self-esteem, and to encourage her to be more open and honest in her relationships in general. And, what's more she has avoided the frustration and repressed anger that often accompany non-assertiveness.

In the assertive training groups we've led during the past several years, we have tried to help promote the attitudes we are encouraging throughout this book. In our groups ten to sixteen women, often of different ages and backgrounds, meet for a two-hour session every week over a six to eight week period. They learn how to communicate assertively; they role play to practice their assertiveness and they share their successes and frustrations.

It's exciting to be a part of their growth, to help women recognize their rights and act on them effectively. Time and again we have watched women succeed, first on a small scale and then on a large one, and almost inevitably they start to view themselves more positively in the process.

Why Is Assertive Training Particularly Important for Women?

We are often asked, "Why assertive training for women?" "Don't men need it too?" Our answer is *yes*. Lots of men benefit from it. But in our society non-assertive behavior is often seen as an asset for women, and they are rewarded for it. "She's so sweet, she never says an unkind word." The same kind of non-assertiveness in men is usually considered a distinct liability. "He's so wishy-washy, he could never do it." So we are likely to find more women than men for whom non-assertive behavior has become a way of life.

Even with today's increased sensitivity to equal rights for both sexes, many people still expect women to be passive and submissive. Men who start to become more assertive are usually encouraged. "He's become so much stronger. It's good to see him standing up for his rights." But women, who have traditionally been praised for being non-assertive, may get mixed reactions as they begin to change. "What's happening to her? All of a sudden she's so independent! And I used to be able to count on her to take care of everything for me."

One of the beginning exercises in our assertive training groups shows just how pervasive these stereotypes are. In the first session we ask the women to call out the adjectives that come to mind when we say "non-assertive woman." Next we ask for adjectives for "non-assertive man," "aggressive woman," and "aggressive man." This chart lists the groups' typical labels:

NON-ASSERTIVE WOMAN	NON-ASSERTIVE MAN	AGGRESSIVE WOMAN	AGGRESSIVE MAN
feminine	feminine	masculine	masculine
gentle	milquetoast	harsh	dominating
agreeable	wishy-washy	pushy	successful
helpful	helpless	bitchy	heroic
gracious	nervous	domineering	capable
nice	weak	obnoxious	strong
self-effacing	a pushover	emasculating	forceful
nurturing	sentimental	uncaring	manly

Although we occasionally hear negative adjectives associated with "non-assertive woman" and positive ones associated with "non-assertive man," the overwhelming majority of responses make it clear that we admire different behavior in men than in women.[1]

So we have a sexual double standard that approves of the behavior of non-assertive women ("typically feminine") and aggressive men ("typically masculine"), while disapproving of the reverse, non-assertive men and aggressive women. If we don't question these norms, we run the danger of perpetuating these values in our own behavior. In our groups we make a point of questioning them. Since most women have been encouraged to be passive rather than assertive, we concentrate on helping women change their behavior from non-assertive to assertive, rather than from aggressive to assertive. We ask each woman to look at her own life to see how she has been encouraged to remain non-assertive.

How are we, as women, influenced by our socialization? How do we learn how to behave and what's expected of us? Although each of us has had different individual experiences, there are common themes running through the biographies of us all.

Imagine yourself as a female fetus. As you sink back into a dark, warm womb world where all is comfort and joy, you might feel a little cramped and need to kick and stretch. If you kick a lot, your parents' friends will say that you're a boy who's in a hurry to get out and make it in the world. If you remain comfortable and move about only occasionally, people will think you are a girl, content to accept the world as it is.

Had you been born a boy, you'd probably have been welcomed warmly, with expectations of either following in Father's footsteps (if they're big ones)

22

or of surpassing him. As a girl, however, your greeting may be more subdued—particularly if you already have an older sister. "Oh, well, maybe we'll try again," Dad might say. "She *is* a pretty little thing."

As an infant you'll probably hear a lot of "Isn't she sweet—and such a *good* baby." Whereas a boy might hear "Will you look at him hold his head up and turn over—that's some strong fellow." As you grow you'll be cuddled and adorned more than if you'd been a boy, who would probably have been treated with more roughhousing and less gentleness. Your tears are viewed indulgently—perhaps even encouraged—by pampering adults.

It's playtime! As a girl, you are more likely to stay inside and play house or school or dress-up or dolls, or go into your own yard and swing, whereas boys are often expected to go outside, climbing, bike riding, pushing, and eventually playing competitive sports.

At storytime you will hear about lazy Mary, frightened Miss Muffet, or empty-headed Bo-Peep. You'll discover Cinderella and Sleeping Beauty and learn that both beautiful heroines—forever young—are waiting to be magically rescued by a high-status male. You'll also hear about Jack jumping over the candlestick or climbing up the beanstalk to subdue the giant. When you're older you'll read many stories that show boys as intelligent, resourceful, and active, while the girls you read about are often passive and domestic—they watch boys do things. You learn that girls give up easily, are late, and cry a lot. You see mothers cooking, cleaning, and caring for babies, while fathers go to work, earn money, achieve. In school you may eventually start to think that good grades may make you unpopular, especially with the boys, who are supposed to be better at everything. You may even develop a fear of success.

In the process of growing up you may have found it advantageous to pout, withdraw, or cry to get what you want. You may have learned to get attention by smiling frequently or acting coy or helpless. You will probably have been told that you "shouldn't be selfish," and this admonition to take care of others' needs before your own will have become second nature. If you have in fact put yourself first, you've learned to feel guilty afterward, in contrast to boys, who can assert themselves, say what they want—and even fight to get it! You learn to avoid conflict and suppress anger; you're told "Don't rock the boat" and "You catch more flies with honey than with vinegar."

If you go to college it is likely that you will major in the humanities, arts, education, or nursing, rather than in science, mathematics, or pre-professional subjects. Although favorite professors may tell you that you're terrific and can be anything you want, after graduating with honors in English the first question you will be asked in job interviews is "How fast can you type."[2]

This imaginary life history takes you—and so many women—only to early adulthood, as we approach the magic moment of marrying and living happily ever after. That's what so much of our preparation has been for.

So here we are, adult women who have been taught from infancy on to be "feminine"—passive, self-effacing, adaptable, coy, and dependent—often at the expense of subordinating our own needs to those of others. We have learned our non-assertiveness early.

Our passivity and self-effacement are reinforced as we grow up; we carry these traits into adulthood as part of our feminine legacy.

We are in the midst of a revolution, stimulated by the women's movement, that is questioning this legacy and the whole social structure that perpetuates it. In addition to being somebody's daughter, somebody's wife, somebody's mother, somebody's employee, women today are becoming Somebody—aware of themselves as persons in their own right. Women are, in fact, going to work in ever-increasing numbers in traditional and non-traditional fields. Even if a woman doesn't want to be a jockey, a truck driver, or a stockbroker, the women's movement and its legal and social consequences have created greater job opportunities, so that women have more freedom of choice.

Although many women's lives are not touched by all this, some women are demanding equal pay for equal work—and some women are even getting it. Some are finding it easier to get credit and to rent apartments in their own names. Along with these changes in their work and legal standing, many women are assessing their personal relationships from a new perspective. Some are making changes in these relationships, redefining the ways they relate to men, to other women, to their children. Although the process of evaluation and change is often slow, there is a new climate which encourages more variety in life styles, job choices, and role expectations for women than ever before in our nation's history.

Although new options are becoming available, the old feminine conditioning still persists. Assertive training can help to bridge the gap between the old patterns and the new opportunities. For too long the emphasis of many traditional therapists and counselors has been to help women *adjust* and *adapt* to the situations in which they are living—which has often meant that women have been encouraged to be passive, submissive, accommodating others' desires while repressing their own.

If women are going to *change*, rather than adjust, they need some tools. Assertive training is such a tool, and an extremely effective one. It contrasts dramatically with the sorts of counseling and conditioning for passivity to which women traditionally have been exposed.

Assertive training does not focus on a woman's inner psyche, trying to figure out why she feels depressed or inadequate. Rather, it focuses on behavior and how we can change it. *As an active force, assertive training goes beyond the process of consciousness-raising, by preparing women to act on what they recognize as problems.* As we act assertively, openly, and learn to stand up for our rights, our self-confidence is likely to increase and to become part of a self-perpetuating cycle of independence and strength.

Is it possible, we may wonder, to retain the valuable elements of our training as women—intuition, sensitivity, nurturance—and still fulfill ourselves as human beings in a complex world that demands more than just these qualities? Can we keep these enjoyable and undervalued elements of womanhood and, in addition, develop other qualities in order to become people who are also effective, strong, and independent? The answer is a resounding *yes*. Today's world cannot be divided into two halves, the solvers and the soothers. We all need to be both.

How Did You Learn to Be Non-Assertive?

One way to become aware of how we may have learned to be non-assertive is to examine the "messages"—explicit and implicit—from our parents or other significant people in our childhood who told us how to behave. Since much non-assertiveness is an attempt to avoid conflict, a recognition of how our families taught us to deal with conflict may be useful. Some questions to consider are:

1. How did my family handle conflict?
2. How did my parents tell me or train me to deal with conflict? What were their "messages"? (For example: Don't rock the boat. Now, no back talk. Nice girls don't fight. Be pleasant or go to your room. Don't yell. Give it to your little brother. Now, not another word. Be a good girl. Nice girls don't argue/talk back. Children should be seen and not heard. Act sweet/cute/pretty/like a lady. If you make an ugly face, it'll freeze that way and you'll look angry forever.)
3. Did they give my brothers the same messages?
4. How do I deal with conflict now?
5. In what ways, if any, did I learn to get what I wanted without asking for it directly?
6. How do I still use those ways today to get what I want?

Examples of Non-Assertive, Assertive, and Aggressive Behavior

The alternative answers to the following examples indicate possible non-assertive, assertive, or aggressive responses to given situations.

A. You and Jessica are co-workers in an office. Jessica asks you to give her a ride home every evening from now on. You don't want to do it. So you answer:

1. "Well . . . uh . . . I guess I could . . . [pause] . . . Uh . . . O.K." (*Non-assertive:* non-verbal pauses, with apparent hesitancy)

2. "I'd love to take you, but sometimes I have to stop at the market on the way home. And sometimes I leave late." (*Non-assertive:* excuses)

3. "What's the matter? Haven't you and Norman gotten around to buying that second car yet?" (*Aggressive:* sarcastic)

4. "You've got a lot of nerve! Do you think I have nothing better to do than chauffeur you around?" (*Aggressive:* attempt to make the requester feel guilty)

5. "I know it's a pain to wait around for Norman to pick you up, but I'd rather not be tied down to giving you a ride every night. I'd be happy to do it once a week, though." (*Assertive:* compromise)

6. "I understand that you don't like having to wait for Norman to pick you up every night, but I really don't want to be tied down to having to take you." (*Assertive:* direct refusal)

B. It's your lunch hour. You're sitting in a restaurant waiting for a friend. She breezes in a half-hour late, sits down, and without any reference to her late arrival asks, "How are you?" You answer:

1. "Fine, thanks," said with a smile. (*Non-assertive:* denial of actual feelings)

2. "O.K., I guess," said with a frown on your face. (*Non-assertive:* attempt to communicate the real message, but indirectly)

3. "What do you mean, how am I? How do you think I am, sitting here, waiting for you and staring at the ceiling? Do you ever stop to think of anyone but yourself?" (*Aggressive:* an attempt to humiliate the latecomer)

4. "Well, I'd been looking forward to our lunch, but since I've been waiting so long, I've really gotten upset. Now we'll have only a half-hour together." (*Assertive:* a direct statement of feelings)

C. Just as you're about to go out the door, Anna calls you on the telephone. She starts to tell you about the problem she's been having with her parents. You're anxious to get off the phone. You say:

1. "I'd like to hear more about it later. I was just on my way out when you called. I'll call you back tonight." (*Assertive:* direct statement of wishes)

2. "Look, I'm too busy to talk to you now. You've always got some little problem, and I have more important things to do. Good-bye." (*Aggressive:* disregard of the other's wishes and feelings)

3. You listen . . . and listen . . . and listen . . . (*Non-assertive:* accommodation of the other's needs at the expense of your own)

D. You're standing at the blouse counter. The saleswoman says, "Who's next?" It is your turn. The woman next to you says, "I am." You turn to her and

1. smile. (*Non-assertive:* accommodation of the other's needs at the expense of your own)
2. frown silently. (*Non-assertive:* attempt at indirect communication of your wishes)
3. mutter under your breath, "Some people are so pushy"—but you say nothing aloud or directly to anyone. (*Non-assertive:* repression of your own wishes)
4. say, "I believe I was here before you." (*Assertive:* direct expression of your own wishes)
5. say, "No you're not. I was here first. You can't take advantage of me, lady." (*Aggressive:* hostile overreaction)

E. You're at a community meeting. A man speaks up and urges the voters not to appropriate money for a day-care center. He gives inaccurate information in his attempt to persuade people that there is no need for such a facility. You disagree with his ideas and his data. You
1. stand up and say, "I've heard what you have to say and I disagree with you. I would like you to listen to my point of view." (*Assertive:* stand up for legitimate rights without violating the other's rights)
2. stand up and say, "You're a liar. You don't know what you're talking about." (*Aggressive:* intent to humiliate)
3. say nothing to anyone. (*Non-assertive:* refrain from expressing your own opinion)
4. stand up and say, "I don't know much about this. I'm no expert, just a mother, but . . ." (*Non-assertive:* self-demeaning and self-deprecating)
5. whisper to the person sitting next to you about how stupid the speaker is. (*Non-assertive:* indirect, inhibited behavior)

As these examples indicate, there are many different ways of being non-assertive, assertive, and aggressive. Our non-assertive behavior may be total silence, or stating what we want in a way that says, "Don't pay attention to me" or "Don't take me seriously." Or we may non-assertively convey our message to a third party, rather than confront someone directly. We may convey one message in words but a contradictory one non-verbally. We may mask a refusal with excuses instead of being direct.

Likewise, aggressive behavior can take a variety of forms, ranging from open hostility and rudeness, to sneering sarcasm to an attempt to dominate and put down one's antagonist.

The assertive behavior which we have illustrated is direct and honest, whether it is a refusal, a request, or a statement of feelings. In all cases, it is expressed directly to the person with whom we want to communicate. It may include compromise, negotiation, or an empathic way of letting the other person know we've heard her.

2

Everywoman's Bill of Rights

THE kind of rights that we are going to talk about are personal ones: the right to self-expression, the right to seek fulfillment and to be treated with respect. These are not the kind of rights that can be legislated. Can you imagine picketing for the right to set your own priorities or say *no* to someone without feeling guilty?

But these rights are easily overlooked—sometimes by ourselves, and sometimes by those who want to get their way at our expense. When we act non-assertively we are likely to ignore our rights altogether, or knowingly let them be violated. An important goal of assertive training is to learn to believe in our rights so that we will be more likely to assert ourselves and feel good about doing it. Here is a list of what we consider some of the basic rights of all women.

Everywoman's Bill of Rights

1. The right to be treated with respect
2. The right to have and express your own feelings and opinions
3. The right to be listened to and taken seriously
4. The right to set your own priorities
5. The right to say *no* without feeling guilty

6. The right to ask for what you want
7. The right to get what you pay for
8. The right to ask for information from professionals
9. The right to make mistakes
10. The right to choose not to assert yourself

There are lots of other rights you might want to think about: the right to change your mind, to say "I don't know the answer," to say "I need some time to think that over." You might want to add these to your own bill of rights, but for the moment we are going to concentrate on the ones we've listed.

1. The right to be treated with respect

This is the most basic of our personal rights. But we can't expect to be treated with respect unless we believe we deserve it. This may mean throwing off decades of conditioning, but once we start respecting ourselves it is surprising how quickly others begin to respond. Believing that we have the right to be respected paves the way to asserting ourselves when it comes to all our other rights.

June talked about this problem in one of our assertive training groups. "For several years I've been the patient of an obstetrician-gynecologist at a large medical center. The open waiting area is very public, and is often filled with more men and children than with women patients. Yet the nurse calls you to her desk and in a loud voice asks all sorts of personal questions: 'Do you use birth control? If not, why don't you? When did you go on the pill? Or do you use other methods? What? When was your last period? Do you have any particular problems? Are you pregnant? Why have you come here?'

"So *everyone* waiting can hear what you're discussing—and sometimes the kids mimic what you say. I was particularly annoyed on the last visit when the nurse told me, in her usual penetrating voice, to go to the 'little girls' room' and leave a specimen. A four-year-old asked his father what she meant, and the man explained it to the boy in a very loud voice.

"Another thing that bothers me," said June, "is that no one there ever calls me 'Mrs. St. Clair.' It's always 'June'—but patients are expected to call the doctors and the staff by their titles.

"I resent having my privacy invaded. I'm entitled to respect as a human being—and I'm not getting it. In fact, I've become so angry that even though I have great confidence in my doctor, *I simply will not go back to that waiting room.*"

The group pointed out to June that if her doctor was really good she might be throwing the baby out with the bathwater—that instead of taking her feelings out on herself, she might be more satisfied in the long run if she complained directly to the doctor and the nurse about the lack of respect shown to her in the waiting room. After she had calmed down, she agreed to try it.

The next week June told us that she had called her doctor and explained how she felt. He had agreed that the crowded conditions were less than ideal and he also said that he would be angry too if he had been treated that way. He promised to talk to the nurse right away to see what could be done about the problem, and thanked June for talking this over with him since he felt that if it were bothering June so much it was probably bothering other patients too.

2. The right to have and express your own feelings and opinions

If you concentrated on twenty-eight-year-old Rachel's widely set green eyes, handsome handcrafted jewelry, and wry sense of humor you tended to forget that she was slightly overweight. But she was not being humorous when she described to the assertive training group a party that she had attended on the previous weekend. She had just begun to feel comfortable with the dozen or so strangers in the small apartment when Donna, the only person she knew, began.

"Hey, I thought you weren't supposed to eat sweets." She pointed at Rachel's half-devoured chocolate cake.

"I know it, but I couldn't resist. It looks so good."

"Rachel, you must be Weight Watchers' worst failure."

Rachel didn't answer and pretended not to notice, but her face flushed with embarrassment as she defiantly kept on eating. The life had gone out of the party for Rachel. She left early, with a headache.

The next morning she decided that, rather than let her resentments build up, she would be assertive and tell Donna that she didn't like to be teased and wanted her to stop. So she calmly told Donna how she felt and what she wanted.

But Donna replied, "Oh, Rachel, you know I wouldn't hurt you for the world! But sometimes I think you're too sensitive. I mean, sometimes a person's so touchy that they miss out on a lot of fun. Look at you right now—you're so uptight and rigid. I'm sorry I hurt you, but you know . . . you really shouldn't feel that way. [Laughs.] If only you'd seen

35

the look on your face last night when you were eating that chocolate cake! [Laughs again.]"

So Rachel was put down again. She said, "Maybe you're right." But inside she was seething and ready to explode. What had gone wrong? She had asserted herself, just as she knew she had the right to do. But now Donna was telling her she shouldn't have felt the way she felt, and Rachel was feeling even worse than before.

Donna had switched her tactics. Initially, her teasing had infringed on Rachel's basic right to be treated with respect. When Rachel confronted her with this Donna, after briefly acknowledging and apologizing for the teasing, went on to infringe on Rachel's rights again, *redefining the issue* by telling Rachel that it was wrong of her to be so easily wounded. *Donna denied Rachel's rights to have and express her own feelings.*

To escape Donna's trap, Rachel could have persevered in insisting on her own rights. She could have said, emphatically, that whether or not Donna considered it appropriate, she was, in fact, sensitive about being overweight. She was acknowledging this and trying to cope with her own feelings by asking Donna not to tease her. If Donna had persisted in arguing, Rachel could have emphasized that she has a right to her feelings.

In the group we role-played the situation, and it went something like this:

RACHEL: Donna, I don't like you to tease me. I know you apologized for it, but right now you're telling me to stop being so sensitive. I *do* have this sore spot, and I'm angry that you're telling me I shouldn't have it.

DONNA: Oh, come on—can't you take a little joke?

RACHEL [with a mixture of hurt and anger]: *You* may think it's just a little joke, but it's not the least bit funny to me.

DONNA: How could anyone feel so strongly about such a little thing? I wouldn't deliberately hurt you.

RACHEL: Donna, I know you aren't trying to hurt me on purpose, but I do feel strongly about being teased, and I'd like you to stop it.

DONNA: O.K. If that's the way you feel . . .

RACHEL: Yes, it really is.

Believing that we have a *right* to our own feelings is a new experience for many of us. We may have learned from early childhood how to be agreeable, to pretend that we're having fun even if we aren't, to be a good sport by going along with the crowd. The implicit message in this training teaches us to deny our own feelings, and if we do this often enough we may begin to forget what our feelings are. Moreover, the denial of feelings and the right to express them may hinder the pleasure and intimacy of close relationships that would have thrived in an atmosphere of openness and honesty.

When we do express our own feelings, it is important to remember to *take responsibility for them.* If we say, for instance, "*You* make me feel hurt when you tease me about being overweight," we are blaming the other person and putting her on the defensive.

On the other hand, we could say, "I get upset when you tease me about my weight. So I'd like you to stop it." In this case, we are accepting the responsibility for our own feelings and expressing our own wishes. *We are neither blaming nor labeling the other person.* We are acting on our right to express our feelings openly. Then it is up to the teaser to choose to acknowledge or ignore our request.

3. *The right to be listened to and taken seriously*

Joyce told our group of a dinner-party conversation she'd recently had with an apparently affable man, Ted, which went as follows:

TED: Hey, I hear you're taking a course in assertive training. What's it all about?

JOYCE: Well, I guess you could say it's a combination of learning to believe in our rights to express ourselves and getting some specific skills to do it. And—

TED [interrupts]: Assertive training for *women*, though. It seems to me that the last thing in the world we need to have is more angry women stomping around!

JOYCE: Wait a minute. There's a difference between *assertive* and *aggressive* behavior—

TED [interrupts again, smirking]: Oh, you're really serious about this, aren't you? You women look so cute when you're all fired up about this women's lib stuff. But honestly—assertive training? Why do you need something like that? Tell me more about it. Maybe I'm missing the point.

JOYCE: Look, Ted, I don't like being told I look cute when I'm in the middle of explaining something important. If you really want to talk about assertive training and hear what I have to say, fine. Then I'd be happy to discuss it with you—but minus the sarcasm.

TED: Aw, come on. Sure I'd like to hear what you have to say. But you must admit—assertive train-

ing for women—the talkers of the human race?
I mean, you have to agree that it *is* a little funny.
I can't believe you're really serious about it.

JOYCE: Well, I am serious, and I don't feel as though
you're willing to believe that. So let's drop it for
now.

This conversation triggered intense feelings in almost every woman in the group. They began to share incidents in which they had been put down by humor or sarcasm.

"It's a tactic," one woman explained. "Sometimes when people find your ideas or actions threatening, they use sarcasm as a way of not having to deal seriously or directly with you. It's a put-down, it's aggressive."

Another added, "Congratulations on behaving so assertively. You didn't fall into Ted's trap; you didn't get defensive, and didn't stop taking yourself seriously or asking Ted to respect your opinions."

A third woman said, "I think this is a woman's issue. Can you imagine a man saying to another man in an argument, 'Oh, you're so cute when you're mad'?"

Everyone agreed that Joyce had set a good example for their future behavior by taking herself seriously.

4. The right to set your own priorities

Marjorie, a distinguished-looking widow, liked her job in a dress store. But her work schedule left her little free time and energy, and she hoarded both. Claire, a neighbor in the next apartment building, called just as Marjorie had finished showering and was settling in for the evening, and said, "I haven't

39

seen you in ages, and we've all missed you. How would you like to play bridge tonight?"

Marjorie replied, "Not tonight, Claire. I'm tired, and I just want to collapse and watch a re-run of *The African Queen* on T.V."

"You know, you need a little enjoyment in your life. You never go out any more," answered Claire, as sweet as molasses, and as sticky.

"Claire, I appreciate your calling, but I've been on my feet all day, and I feel like being alone and resting." Marjorie drew her robe tighter and got ready to hang up.

Claire pressed on. "Well, this will give you a chance to sit down—"

"No, really—"

Claire continued, over the protest. "Come on, Marj. You're not doing anything. We're trying to get a game together and we need a fourth . . . No, we couldn't get anyone else. There're three of us, and we need one more person. If you don't come you'll spoil our game . . . Yes, we just *have* to play tonight. No, tomorrow won't do. You're the *only* one who can help us. And we always have such a good time when you're playing."

"Well, all right." Marjorie hung up the phone, barely restraining herself from slamming down the receiver. As she dressed, and throughout the evening, she became more and more resentful of what she considered Claire's steamroller tactics and attempts to make her feel guilty.

Although Marjorie may have believed intellectually that she had the right to decide how to use her own time, she let herself be talked out of it.

Marjorie had other alternatives. After the initial invitation and refusal, when Claire intensified the pressure, Marjorie could have said, "Yes, I certainly understand what a problem it will be if you can't find a fourth, but I still won't be coming tonight. I'd be happy to have you ask me again some other time when I'm not so tired."

In this instance, Marjorie would be showing an understanding of Claire's situation, yet she would also be making it clear that she has a right to set her own priorities.

5. *The right to say* no *without feeling guilty*

Marilyn, a mother of four children under eight, told our assertive training group about a consistent problem. Her husband, a salesman, was often out of town, and she was home a great deal. She was constantly being asked to help other people out—with nursery school, with PTA, with car pools, with babysitting other children, with plant watering for neighbors on vacations, with Tupperware parties, with collections for worthy causes.

"Sometimes," she said, "I say *yes* because either the activity sounds like fun or the cause is worthwhile, or because I want to be helpful."

Then she frowned. "Most of the time I say *yes* because I can't think of a good reason to say *no* and I'd feel guilty if I refused. Even worse, at other times I *do* say *no* and feel terribly guilty afterwards. For instance, three weeks ago Doris, my neighbor, said, 'Marilyn, could you possibly help me out this year? I'm in a terrible bind because for years I canvassed the neighborhood for cancer research, but this year the only time that Jerry could take his vacation is during the solicitation time, and we'll be in Florida.'

"I tried to give her an excuse, saying I wouldn't

41

have time to be away from the kids, but she kept right on talking: 'Oh, don't worry about leaving your kids—they can go with you. The neighbors always give more money if a child holds the can, and my kids love it. And your children are so cute—especially the baby.' Doris talked harder and faster. 'Both of us are so lucky to have healthy children, it's the least we can do, don't you think? If you've ever seen children in the hospital you know what I mean. I'm sure you won't mind doing it for such an important cause.'"

Marilyn continued, "I stood there shaking my head, but she said, 'And I've seen you walking with your children lots of times. You could just do it when you're out with them anyway.'

"So I finally said *yes*. It was easier to do that than to feel guilty. I did it, but my heart wasn't in it, and I know I didn't collect as much money as I should have—I missed a lot of people. I just hated doing it, and I know that's why I haven't been to see Doris since she got back from Florida. I'm too angry at her, and that's unreasonable. Yet I feel she conned me into doing that collection, and even though I approve of the charity, I don't like collecting for it."

When the other members of the group said that they wouldn't have minded soliciting for that worthy cause, we suggested that for them Doris's request would not have provoked a situation calling for assertion. They would have been doing what they chose to do.

But for Marilyn, who did not want to collect, the situation clearly called for an assertive act. A firm and clear refusal to seek donations could have forestalled the unpleasant consequences. "I might have felt guilty, though," she said.

"But how do you feel now—about yourself and about Doris?" we asked. "You don't want to feel guilty, but now you feel angry at yourself and resentful of Doris, and probably even a little guilty for not doing a thorough job of collecting."

Marilyn certainly would have kept her relationship with Doris on a more honest basis if she'd said *no*. She could have preceded her refusal with an indication that she understood how hard it was to find people to canvass, and she could have sympathized with Doris's problem even though she wasn't going to be the one to solve it.

Finally Marilyn decided to try out saying *no* when it suited her needs, hoping that it would get easier each time. Chances are it would get easier with each successful *no*, and she'd become less anxious about trying it again.

6. The right to ask for what you want (knowing that others have the right to refuse)

Many women are afraid to ask for what they want for fear of being turned down. If you are staying in a hotel and are assigned a room on a busy street, you certainly have the right to request a room in a quieter part of the hotel. You may or may not get it, but you can be sure of *not* getting it if you don't ask for it.

Women may not make requests for fear of appearing ignorant, or of imposing themselves. It is perfectly acceptable, in most circumstances, to admit that we need help. As for imposing ourselves, the other person can always refuse our request.

7. The right to get what you pay for

Here we are talking about assertiveness in pursuing the rights to which we're entitled as consumers of goods or services. If we ask for our hair to be cut very short, we're entitled to have it cut as we want. If we hire a babysitter, we have the right to expect our children to be cared for according to our instructions.

It was after Thanksgiving when Sherry, a federal employee, told our group of a prolonged encounter with Mr. Jenkins, the manager of her apartment building. When she first rented it, in the summer, she was unaware of any problems, but as the weather turned cold in late October, so did her lodging. During the first week when her apartment temperature never rose above sixty-two degrees, Sherry asked the manager for more heat. He said there was nothing he could do; the fault had to be in her reaction to the weather. After all, no one else in the building was complaining. And Sherry said no more.

Her concern grew as she grew colder and colder, so she shared the problem with the assertive training group, which urged her to assert her rights with Mr. Jenkins. Anticipating indifference, or even a hard time, Sherry nevertheless went home, knocked on his door, and explained her problem:

SHERRY: I've been cold now for a week. The radiators aren't giving off heat, and I'd like to have them fixed soon, since the cold season's starting.

MR. JENKINS: Well, are you sure it's too cold? I haven't had any other gripes.

SHERRY: You probably haven't. Evidently the problem is in my apartment radiators. However, it's usually between sixty degrees and sixty-two degrees,

and that's too cold for me. I would like you to
have the radiators fixed.

MR. JENKINS: How do you know it's that cold? Maybe
your thermometer's broken, not your radiators.

SHERRY: My thermometer isn't broken. I'm cold, and
I'd like the radiators fixed.

MR. JENKINS: O.K., O.K., I'll have George, my repair-
man, come in and check them.

Another week went by, and no one came. Sherry
was more hesitant in approaching Mr. Jenkins this
time, for she had already done so twice with no satisfaction. However, she thought through what her rights
were in this situation, and knew that since the heat
was included in her rent, she had a right to get what
she was paying for. So her next dialogue with Mr.
Jenkins went as follows:

SHERRY: As I recall, two weeks ago you agreed to
have someone fix the radiators, and no one has
come yet. My apartment is still too cold.

MR. JENKINS: Oh, I forgot to tell you. I called George,
and he said it would be a while before he could
come. Those guys are busy—especially at this
time of year.

SHERRY: Your maintenance person may be busy. But
my apartment is getting colder and more uncomfortable by the minute, and I don't want to
wait much longer for repairs.

MR. JENKINS: Well, I'll call again, but don't expect
miracles.

SHERRY: I appreciate your checking on it again. But
since it has already taken so long, how about if
we set a time limit of three more days? If George
can't promise it, I would like you to call someone else. Either that, or I'll get another repair-

45

person myself and deduct the cost from my next month's rent.

MR. JENKINS: Well, I never let anyone but George handle the repairs. He's the only one who knows this heating system, and it's him or no one. I'll try hard, but I can't promise.

SHERRY [firmly]: Well, I'll check back tomorrow. If George can't come within three days, I'll try to find someone who can get here sooner, and deduct the cost from the rent. It's much too cold in the apartment.

With this promise, Sherry left, feeling much better about herself. She realized that the situation could have dragged on and on, but by asserting herself some time limits had been set for the manager to make good on his word. If he didn't, Sherry would simply take action on her own, in spite of his objections.

Closely related to this right is the next right.

8. The right to ask for information from professionals

As medical or dental patients, we have a number of significant rights. We may hesitate to enforce them for fear of offending the doctor or because we've grown up in awe of these professionals. Nevertheless, assertive training can help to change our perspective and enable us to overcome our reluctance to ask for all the information we're entitled to.

As patients, we have the right to ask doctors for various sorts of information about our own bodies, and about the prescribed treatment.

We have the right to ask and receive answers to the following questions:

- What is the general and specific condition of my health?
- What are the results of any routine tests made on me?
- What are the results of any diagnostic tests? For what purposes were they conducted?
- With what medication or other form(s) of therapy am I being or going to be treated? Why? What are the long- and short-range goals of this treatment? What are its advantages? What are its potential side effects? Are there any acceptable alternatives to the prescribed treatment?
- What will your services cost?
- What is the estimated cost of related services (lab tests, X-rays, physical therapy, etc.) not directly performed or billed by your office?

Whether or not the practitioner's answers to the above are satisfactory, we also have other rights. Among them are:

- The right to arrange for a consultation with another specialist
- The right to communicate our concerns to the people who will be treating us
- The right to request that a faulty or inadequate service be done over again at no extra cost to ourselves
- The right, as clients of professionals, to be treated with respect and confidentiality

Judging from our assertive training groups, many of us find it very hard to assert ourselves sufficiently to take advantage of these rights.

All these rights are perfectly justifiable. Thoughtful, reliable practitioners should be sympathetic to

47

such requests anyway, and may even anticipate some of them. If not, you might want to consider changing doctors. After all, we're their patients, and this is their job.

Not only do we have medical rights, we have the right to know what *services* lawyers, bankers, accountants, educators, counselors, social workers, and other professionals will perform, and *in what manner, over what period of time*, and *at what cost*. We also have the right to be told, clearly, what professionals *cannot or will not do*, and at what point we might need to arrange for additional services from someone else. Obviously, these rights apply to our relations with trades and service people too.

9. The right to make mistakes

Nobody's perfect. We may think nothing of it when someone else makes a mistake, but then turn around and become very hard on ourselves when we do it. Learning any new skill takes practice, and by its nature practice involves making mistakes. To grow we have to experiment and take risks—especially now that we have so many new options as women.

We can stop ourselves from growing if we take an "I must be perfect" attitude. Give yourself a break. Take the risk of saying what you think, even though you may be wrong. We have the right to make mistakes, and so does everyone else.

10. The right to choose not to assert yourself

A friend suggested that we call our book *Being Assertive Is Knowing When to . . .*—and, we might add, *When Not to*. We have already discussed the fact that having assertive skills does not necessarily solve all our problems.

We can realistically try to determine when being assertive might backfire and cause more difficulties than it would solve. If a situation is dominated by others with power who are concerned with maintaining it at all costs, then an individual assertion could well be either an exercise in futility or a disaster. In such lopsided situations, it is usually better to assess the possible consequences and then decide whether asserting yourself is worth the risk.

We may sometimes decide not to pursue our rights, even though we feel we are entitled to them. If, for example, asking your chain-smoking boss to stop smoking in a meeting might jeopardize your relationship with him, you might decide it's not a good idea. Sometimes one priority outweighs another. Then, too, there are times when asserting ourselves just doesn't seem worth the effort. You might be in a hurry, the other person just may not matter enough to you, or you may be just plain tired.

And finally we should consider when it is appropriate to assert our rights and when it isn't.

I may have the right to express my opinion, but do I have the right to do so in a loud voice during a film or theater performance? What about the rights of the rest of the audience to get what they've paid for (a performance they can hear)? Do I have the right to be listened to if I keep talking long after the other person has obviously lost interest? Doesn't the listener have the right to set his own priorities? What about the other person's right to be treated with respect?

At times one person's rights may conflict with another's. In a communal living situation, Helen may decide that her priorities include sharing of all possessions and space with the other people in her household. At what point will her behavior start infringing on the rights of others? Helen has the right to tell them what her beliefs and priorities are, and the right to ask for a fair hearing. But she does not have the right to expect that her living companions will necessarily adopt her priorities or want to live by them.

In asserting our rights it is always important to remember that other people have rights too. Just as it is important to be straightforward, it is also important to be flexible.

3

Games Women Play
to Avoid Asserting Themselves

IT *is unfortunate that we live in a culture that promotes various types of hypocrisy, that discourages personal openness, that favors numerous social inhibitions, and that upholds a tradition of personal dishonesty in the name of tact or considerateness. Within these corruptive confines, women have the doubly demanding task of skillfully playing these nefarious societal games while pretending to be stupid at the same time.*[3]

The games[4] which many of us have been taught and encouraged to play are exercises in non-assertive behavior. We may have been taught, directly or indirectly that if we come right out and say what we want, we will antagonize others and they probably will like us less. So, fearful of the unknown results of openness and honesty, and imagining the worst, we often find ways to escape our own anxiety by avoiding directness with others. Yet because our needs remain, despite their suppression, we may resort to various indirect and manipulative ways of obtaining them.

Obviously, men too can and do use indirect techniques to avoid assertion; these are not necessarily sex-related ploys. However, because of the emphasis of *The New Assertive Woman*, we will discuss these from a woman's point of view, and describe some of the games so many of us play.

Games, as we define them, are manipulative and dishonest. They include covert, ambiguous, and indirect and unclear communication. These indirect techniques follow a patterned series of moves on the part of the principal player. Often the player herself is unaware that she's playing.

At times she may be rewarded for her game playing—with approval, with cooperation, and by getting her way. If the game player does get what she wants, she's likely to be pleased by the short-range benefits of such success and play the game again—and perhaps again and again.

But despite these seeming advantages, games are likely to be unsatisfying to all but the principal player, and often even to her, for the ultimate results can be costly. Through relying on indirect, manipulative means of trying to get what she wants, the player is left *vulnerable and dependent on others to pick up her hints and clues as to what she means and wants.* She also *runs the risk of being misinterpreted.* Because game playing rests on the shaky assumption that others will continue to respond to our tactics as we expect them to, *the initiator relinquishes her power to control her own communication.*

Games are unnecessary, as we will illustrate, for assertive behavior can provide a positive option for us all.

GAME I
The Sufferer, or "After all I've done for you"

When a person becomes The Sufferer, she tries to evoke enough sympathy for her plight so that someone will feel obligated to rescue her without her ever having to ask for help directly. As part of the suffering, she may end up doing the work that others refuse to do and attending to their wishes while subordinating her own. She usually resents this.

A sufferer tries to get what she wants by sending indirect messages. She may act overworked, persecuted, or totally dependent. Or she may try to look put-upon, sigh a lot, and utter indirect complaints. She is trying to say, "If you appreciated—or even noticed—all the things I do for you, all the sacrifices I make, you'd automatically want to do more for me."

However, suffering strategies often backfire. This self-denying behavior may actually encourage others to take for granted that part of our function is to serve them—*at our own expense*. They expect service, and we provide it. This is not a very rewarding position to be in. Another way this can backfire is when the people who are not being dealt with honestly start to feel more resentment than pity toward the sufferer, and seek to withdraw from the game once they realize that they are being manipulated.

What is the assertive alternative to suffering? State your goals openly, identify your limits, and figure out what you would like from others. And always remember that other people have rights too. If your exchange of views is open, honest, and caring, you will probably reach satisfactory solutions without too much trouble. Even if you don't get what you asked for, at least your requests are out in the open, and the refusal is less likely to be taken as a personal rejection. And in the long run you'll probably find that people are more likely to cooperate willingly if their help is asked for in a straightforward way, rather than through some devious means that shames them into chivalry.

GAME II
Uninvolved, or "It doesn't matter to me,
whatever you want"

JOHN [on the telephone]: Are you busy tonight? How about going to a movie?

ALICE [hesitating]: Well, I guess that's O.K. [She had been planning to go shopping after work and then come home and wash her hair.] Yes . . . that would be fun [weakly], I suppose.

JOHN: What would you like to see?

ALICE [softly]: Oh, it really doesn't make any difference.

JOHN: We could see the new Fellini film downtown, or we could just zip over to the Varsity and see the western.

ALICE: Whichever you prefer. [She hates westerns.]

JOHN: I don't feel like driving all the way downtown, so let's go to the Varsity.

ALICE [long pause, followed by a sigh]: Well . . . O.K.

JOHN: Are you sure that's what you want?

ALICE: It doesn't really matter that much—whatever you like.

When we choose to stay uninvolved and give up our part in making choices, it is often because of the mistaken belief that expressing an opinion will antagonize others. If we are too anxious about making straightforward requests, we may resort to indirect ways of manipulating situations to get what we want. The strategies of Staying Uninvolved include refraining from initiating behavior that requires decision-making, always deferring to what others want, and never expressing our own opinion.

To avoid giving an opinion is to *avoid responsibility for the course that the action takes,* for any *conflicts* it may present, and for its *outcome.* "Don't blame me. I had nothing to do with it." "Everybody else was doing it." "I knew it would be a terrible movie, but *you* wanted to see it."

The deliberately uninvolved person is *never wrong* —and *never right*. She *never takes the risks* of being assertive and using her power—and she never experiences the satisfaction of being responsible for getting what she wants when she does get it. But in trying to avoid antagonizing others, she may end up irritating them even more than she would have by being straightforward. Her refusal to accept the blame for undesired consequences may also antagonize. Moreover, if she really does have an opinion, denying it is dishonest, not to mention frustrating.

A woman who wants to Stay Uninvolved may also rationalize away her wants by discounting their value. "It's silly of me to want that." "I don't really need it." "After all, I can go out to lunch some other time." "Yes, let Jack have the promotion. It's probably more important to him than it is to me."

Sometimes, in more extreme cases, anxiety about conflict may cause one not only to submerge her own wishes, but to ask others to do the same. When it works, it allows her to soothe ruffled feathers and act as a mediator in arguments. She encourages people to behave, as she does, in ways expressed in a variety of clichés. "Let sleeping dogs lie." "Turn the other cheek." "Don't rock the boat." "Keep smiling." "Look for the silver lining."

This kind of conciliator may drive people away with her maddening optimism and her denial of real feelings. Or others may vent their anger on her. So long as she believes, irrationally, that she is responsible for other people's feelings, she is not likely to consider her own needs.

In all these instances, the game player behaves non-assertively and dishonestly, in that her outward approval of the others' decisions or behavior masks her inner resentment at not getting what she really wants. But she pays a price of internal tensions if she bottles it up. Or she may express anger indirectly but more actively, by taking it out on objects (slamming doors, driving recklessly) or transferring it to other people, the innocent victims of her game.

The obvious alternative to Staying Uninvolved is to express one's own opinion, directly and honestly. When John called, Alice could have admitted that she already had made plans to go shopping. She might then have listened to John's suggestions of movies, and have changed her mind if she honestly preferred the new possibility. If not, she could have thanked him for the invitation but said that she preferred to stick with her original plan. If she really wanted to see John at another time, she could have told him so.

GAME III
The Wet-Blanket, or
"I won't fight
but I won't give you satisfaction, either"

Helen lives in the household of her son, Bob, and daughter-in-law, Emily. Emily wants to redecorate their family room by purchasing woven basket chairs and big pillows which can be used for sitting on the floor. Helen prefers a comfortable couch. The following approach to this problem is sometimes called Passive Resistance.

EMILY: Some of those fabrics on the pillows I saw yesterday are gorgeous.
HELEN: Were they cotton?

EMILY: Yes.

HELEN: They'll probably shrink when you wash them. And they'll show the dirt.

EMILY: Oh, maybe we could look for other kinds of fabric and cover them ourselves.

HELEN: That should be done professionally. Besides, anything that sits around on the floor will start looking terrible soon. [Wearily] But if that's what you want, get them.

EMILY: Well, I like big pillows. Is there anything you particularly want?

HELEN: Not exactly. Furniture should be sensible and made to last. But it's your house. You do what you like. I can always sit in the living room.

Later Helen reported sanctimoniously to a friend that she was not the kind of mother who antagonized her children by bothering them with her opinions or telling them what to do, unless they begged her for advice. Yet Helen did not support anyone else's ideas unless they happened to be the same as hers. This became, implicitly, an either/or proposition: "Either you guess what I want and consider it or I'll resist cooperating until you feel bad or are exasperated enough to ask my opinion and do what I do."

While the resister intends to *avoid conflict,* imagined or real, she also wants to *get her own way,* but without telling the other people what she wants. She *withdraws support for what the others want,* and she may even *refuse to discuss* the reasons for her withdrawal. She may not even acknowledge that it is happening. "Anything you want. It's your house. Do what you like." Often she *points out the flaws* in other people's behavior, without stating what she would like to see changed. She hopes that others will *recognize her dis-*

approval and plead with her to tell them how they might accommodate her.

There are three likely outcomes of Passive Resistance, all unsatisfactory. One is that other people might genuinely miss the game player's oblique message. Although they would not experience any conflict or tension, the resister might become resentful because her own wishes, not having been expressed or recognized, would not have been fulfilled, either. This often happens in a close relationship. "If you really cared about me, you'd know what I want."

Another alternative is that the others may decide that the resister's stakes are too high; the price of her cooperation demands too many concessions from them. So they may ignore her—reasonably easy to do, since she's not overtly stating what she wants. This way they will frustrate her desire to get her own way. And if they should also start to resent her and decide to tell her off, her passive resistance will have provoked the very conflict she sought to avoid.

Then there are those who give in to the manipulator, seeking her opinions and satisfying her desires, but at the cost of their own peace of mind. In the short run the manipulator may get what she wants. But in the long run, because of her dishonest means, she is likely to suffer too—from an increase in her guilt, from a loss of trust, and even from the unhappiness she's caused others who have unwillingly done what she wanted.

The positive alternative to Passive Resistance is open discussion, mutual understanding, and, possibly, compromise or a new solution. Helen could have simply said she preferred a comfortable couch. However, she should also have considered Emily's rights and feelings, as well as her own. If it had been handled this way, Emily might have agreed to a couch, in which case Helen would have gotten what she wanted, without frustrating Emily.

Or Emily might have disagreed, explaining why she didn't want a couch—but even if Helen didn't get her wish, the tensions resulting from manipulative behavior and confused responses would have been avoided.

All of the maneuvers described so far—Suffering, Staying Uninvolved, and Passive Resistance—could in some instances be seen as possible forms of the next game, which we call Sabotage.

GAME IV
*The Saboteur, or "I'll go through the motions
of doing what you want, but I'll
silently fight your request every step of the way.
If I don't get what I want, watch out—
I may find some way to get even"*

Let's look at three examples of sabotage:

Pat's employers expected all of the secretaries to take turns making coffee and cleaning up. Pat hated to do this, but she was afraid to say so, even though she knew this was the only way to change the situation. She was afraid that her refusal would make the other secretaries mad and she would not be able to cope with their anger.

She didn't refuse to make the coffee every Thursday, her day, but funny things started to happen. The coffee was either too weak or too strong. Sometimes she forgot to make it. Sometimes she forgot to clean up. Sometimes she ran out of supplies. On occasion she developed a headache. She often felt overworked in other respects. Soon she began to make snide remarks about her supervisor, who had thought up the coffee plan. She thought of quitting her job. Instead of discussing what she actually wanted, Pat made the situation miserable for everyone—most of all, for herself.

Jane's husband had been coming home late more and more often. Although he always called to let her know what time he would be arriving, his re-warmed dinners always seemed to turn out badly: They were meager, overcooked, and unappetizing. Jane was expressing her displeasure with Hal by making him pay, rather than talking with him about the problem.

Gerry, a sales clerk, was asked by her department manager to work an extra evening a week for several months. On those evenings her sales totals were markedly below her usual average, and she made numerous bookkeeping errors. She did not tell her boss of her objections to working the extra time, and therefore did not resolve the problem. Instead, she sabotaged.

The Saboteur accommodates others while subordinating her own desires. She wishes to *avoid conflict* or the imagined anger of others if they are confronted directly with her desires. Yet her self-effacing behavior leaves her angry at those she thinks are taking advantage of her. As a result of her frustration, she may "get even" in indirect ways, while simultaneously going through the motions of trying to carry out the others' requests; she hopes that her maneuvers will eventually get her message across or in some way get the others involved enough to recognize what she wants and take care of her without requiring her to be direct or honest.

The Saboteur ostensibly plays by the others' rules. She *does what they want*, usually without verbal protest. But she *makes up her own contradictory rules*, which she also follows. "I'll do it my own way—when I am good and ready—if I remember at all." So her non-assertive behavior is *contradictory* and *self-defeating*. The Saboteur would really like other people to *cancel their demands on her*, but she doesn't dare tell them this directly. So she uses various tactics to covertly undermine their demands. Among these are:

Procrastination. "I'll do it tomorrow"—and *mañana* may or may not come.

Lateness. She's late for events that she doesn't want to attend. So she effects a compromise that satisfies no one. She would have preferred not to go; others would have preferred her to be there for the whole thing. (And her lateness may disrupt the event—an indirect way of expressing her own resentment toward those conducting it.)

Slowdown. By halfheartedly doing the last-minute overtime rush job her boss has imposed on her against her will, she takes much longer and works much less effectively than she does when she wants to do something.

Sloppiness or carelessness. She does the work, but so sloppily that extra effort is required to correct the errors. In some cases the whole project may be so fouled up that it has to be entirely redone or abandoned.

Forgetfulness or neglect. Perhaps the epitome of non-assertive behavior is to deny through forgetfulness the existence of the commitment one made unwillingly but didn't want to keep.

Sometimes Sabotage can involve more conspicuously manipulative behaviors, such as *undermining the per-*

son rather than confronting the situation. The Saboteur may spread rumors, innuendos, or insults about the person(s) whom she considers responsible for the situation she doesn't like. She hopes in this way to get other people on her side and to encourage them to share her resentment. She may try to arouse a champion in her defense who will represent her point of view in discussing the problem with her alleged antagonist. She may even organize an opposition to take action against her antagonist, although she does so without directly and assertively confronting the issue itself.

Sabotage may be more detrimental to the Saboteur than to the other players. Her non-assertive tactics of indirect communication may convey the *wrong message*—that she is incompetent, absent-minded, neglectful, irresponsible, vindictive, disloyal—rather than her own view that the request was unreasonable or the situation undesirable.

Furthermore, she herself rather than her intended victim may bear the brunt of the delays and extra work that her sabotage causes. If she has to work overtime and prolongs the work, it's her time and her extra energy that are being expended, not those of her boss. And she is still doing what she doesn't want to do, and suffering whatever resentments she may have as a result.

Or, if her procrastination, carelessness, forgetfulness, or neglect does inconvenience others, the Saboteur may well anger them anyway—and for a *real* reason, rather than the one that she had imagined. So her non-assertiveness may have caused problems, rather than solving them.

An assertive approach would be to discuss the problem honestly—and immediately—with whoever is responsible for making the demands or is in a position to change the situation. Together they could talk about other ways of handling the problem, and they could consider some compromise. Even if they couldn't find one, at least the points of difficulty would have been confronted directly. Although her aims might be frustrated, the distressed person would at least feel that she had done what she could to solve her problem. Thus, the likelihood of secret resentments would have been minimized, and, one hopes, so would the threat of Sabotage.

GAME V
The Seductress, or
"Poor little me needs
big, strong, handsome you"

There can be a feeling of excitement, mellowness, or intimacy when we're in tune with someone who lets us know it's mutual. The reciprocal appreciation, flattery, and possible flirtation can be fun, and may sometimes lead to a closer relationship with someone else.

However, in the game of Seduction the player uses seductive behavior manipulatively, as a sexual way of obtaining non-sexual goals, such as favors or privileges, without asking for them directly.

Although in our culture men have traditionally been regarded as the seducers, we are talking about the seductive and flirtatious behavior that *women initiate*, primarily in their relationships with men. We recognize that flattery and self-denigration, such as the ploy of "Poor little me needs competent/self-assured you," can be used with other women as well, but here we are concentrating on how we tend to use these ploys with men.

During the past seventy-five years, for example, the Vamp, the risqué Flapper, the Pin-up Girl, the voluptuous but childlike Blonde have been variously held up as models of what a "real woman" should strive to be. Each of these incorporates some aspects of genuinely flirtatious, seductive behavior. Yet, concurrent with the sexual aspects of seductive behavior, women receive considerable cultural encouragement to use seductive behavior for ulterior motives. We see this all the time in popular literature: The female counterspy seduces the hero in order to learn military secrets; the not-so-dumb Blondie flatters Dagwood to get a new hat; the curvaceous model in the ad beckons, "I'm Ginger—fly me!"

Books are still being published that instruct women in manipulation and seduction, partly on the assumption that she will be rewarded in proportion to how well she masters the maneuvers. Thus, she learns how to admire her husband's body, how to compliment him, how to put his tattered ego back together, and how to submit to his leadership. They tell women to graciously "adapt to her husband's way, even though at times she desperately may not want to. He in turn will gratefully respond by trying to make it up to her and grant her desires. He may even spoil her with goodies."[5]

The popularity of these books shows us just how powerful the influence of our culture really is. Women have been taught that their real fulfillment comes from keeping a man happy at any price. But the new insights into our roles are starting to reveal just how self-defeating this kind of manipulative seduction can be.

In the non-assertive game of Seduction, although the Seducer may make an overt request, she does not do so directly. She must embellish it sexually, with coyness or flattery. She resorts to indirect behavior, believing that men dislike direct, open, honest behavior in women, either because they are unaccustomed to it or they can't cope with it, and men are vain, egotistical, and highly susceptible to flattery, because they believe themselves irresistible to women. The logical expectation here is that men, being so vulnerable to flattery, will respond eagerly to whatever wiles a woman decides to use as she wraps them around her little finger.

This kind of thinking is demeaning to both men and women. Seductive maneuvers for avoiding directness are basically dishonest, because they capitalize on the vanities and vulnerabilities of the seduced person for the imagined benefit of the Seducer. In some cases the Seducer may get what she wants, and this success may encourage her to continue her manipulative behavior. However, the Seducer, too, is vulnerable to the possibility that her indirect communication may be misinterpreted. She is sending one message (sexuality, false humility) and expecting an answer to another hidden message on an entirely different subject. She says: "I love being seen with you. You're so attractive." She means: "Take me out to dinner." Consequently, she is at the mercy of someone else's translation of her message, and must be constantly on her toes to keep her signals straight.

Assertive training tries to encourage women to recognize that directness, honesty, and non-manipulativeness are among their strongest and most enduring natural resources. These resources can give women not only the power to maintain their own sense of self-esteem at any age, but also the power to pursue what they want directly, rather than having to wait around hoping that their ploys will pay off.

Conclusion

We have discussed the common games of Suffering, Staying Uninvolved, Passive Resistance, Sabotage, and Seduction, which by their nature are very costly. Obviously the games are seen to have some advantages, or they wouldn't have been played by so many people for so long—but these presumed advantages are usually short-sighted and ultimately self-defeating. Games consume considerable energy in maneuvering for temporary gains—such as avoiding conflict or escaping responsibilities.

In time, though, the old problems are likely to surface again, in the same or more severe form than they were in before the game playing drove them underground. Games put up walls, which usually don't go away by themselves.

Assertive behavior can make games unnecessary. It can provide the environment for clear understanding of yourself and better insight into others, and the opportunity for direct, honest expression. Assertive behavior breaks down the walls.

4

Deciding to Change
May Be the Toughest Part of All

MAKING the decision to change may be the toughest part of all. Change is not easy. It cannot be imposed on anyone by logic, or rhetoric, or a persuasive assertive training leader. The decision to change can come only from ourselves.

In making this decision it is important to think about what we may be giving up if we change, as well as what we will be gaining. Again, we will be focusing on changing from non-assertive to assertive behavior, rather than from aggressiveness to assertiveness, since this has been the main problem of the women in our groups. The questionnaire at the end of the chapter (page 76) is designed to help you decide whether or not you want to change.

Once we have become aware of recurring patterns of non-assertiveness in our own behavior, we need to examine what kinds of reinforcement we are getting for them. Although we might not choose non-assertiveness as an effective behavior, it does have some seeming advantages.

Sometimes non-assertiveness does *help us avoid possible conflict, anger, rejection, or acceptance of responsibility for our feelings.* As one woman said, "Even though I hate myself for not speaking up, my silence seems worthwhile just to keep some peace in the house."

Being non-assertive, *letting others take the lead in initiating and following through, or playing "uninvolved," is also a means of avoiding responsibility.* "It's not my fault that half the people who went on that winter picnic have colds. It wasn't my idea."

By being non-assertive we may *get taken care of or protected by others.* If we play helpless, we may find someone to do most of our asserting for us. A woman who is anxious about questioning the plumber's bill may let her husband ask about it—and even complain. If the plumber gets angry, the husband rather than the wife will bear his wrath.

Although we may cringe at the thought of remaining silent instead of expressing our true feelings, compliments and praise are powerful incentives to keep us conforming to what others expect of us. "You're always so agreeable," or "We can always count on you to go along with the situation."

Another, and perhaps the most powerful, incentive for remaining non-assertive is that it is familiar: We know how the behavior patterns operate, even if we are not wholly comfortable with them. When we're anxious about risking something new which might produce an unknown outcome, we are likely to behave in familiar ways. If the consequences are good, we're lucky. If they're not so good, we may wish they were different but not know how to change them.

So, you might ask, why should we want to change? Are we likely to gain more than we'll lose?

When we ask these questions in our groups, women often tell us that even though they sometimes get what they want by being non-assertive, they don't like the feelings they have about themselves. Here are some of the disadvantages they see in their own non-assertiveness:

- "I know I get a lot of protection, particularly from my husband, but *I lose my own independence.*"
- "I can stay safe and not risk being told my ideas or opinions are no good, but *I give up my power to make decisions.*"
- "*I give up feeling honest.* When I really do have a strong opinion, I withhold it and go along with others so I won't make waves."
- "*When I don't respect my own rights,* others don't respect them either. I stay safe, but *I lose my sense of self-worth,* and *when* that's gone, *others don't value me either.*"
- "When I stay non-assertive for a long period of time, I generally end up by holding things in for so long that I finally explode and take it out on someone. *I give up a lot of the ability to control how I express my feelings.*"
- "*I lose my sense of inner tranquility.* It's ironic— I stay passive to avoid conflict, but the turmoil goes on inside me."
- "In letting others take the lead, *I never give myself the chance to initiate a plan and see it through.*"
- "*I feel so vulnerable.* It seems as if *I always have to depend on others to figure out what I want.*"

Some of the advantages of becoming assertive are: gaining independence, decision-making power, and responsibility for one's own decisions and behavior; increased honesty, tranquility, self-control, self-respect, and respect of others; and the freedom to be direct, rather than having to depend on others to pick up the indirect clues to what we think or want.

Once we have looked at advantages and disadvantages of behavior in this light, we are better able to figure out what is best for us. The pull of the advantages of an assertive future, combined with the push away from non-assertiveness, may propel us toward change.

One last but very important word about change: We don't live in isolation, but in a society that includes patterns of relationships with many other people. People have come to expect certain behavior of us—that's part of their definition of who we are and how they relate to us.

So when one person in a system or relationship starts to become more assertive, other people react. The changes in the individual may cause changes in relationships with others—and those can be threatening. It is particularly important to remember this as we try out new behavior.

During the transition from non-assertiveness to assertiveness, the woman making the change will find the skills of listening and empathy particularly helpful in being aware of how her new behavior is affecting those closest to her.

We must also realize that the change will take time. Just as we need to become comfortable with our new assertiveness, others also need time to adjust to our changing behavior and become comfortable with the new qualities in the relationship.

After the third assertive training session, one woman decided to write down the story of her personal decision to change. She described how as a child her parents and grandparents had helped her define what kind of a person she was and know how she should act in order to get along in the world—primarily in order to fulfill others' expectations of her. She examined how these childhood views had affected her teen-age and adult life.

She then explained many of the insights that had led to her decision to make major changes in her adult life, after over twenty years in the old pattern. She recognized that her childhood decisions had enabled her to cope with the world in which she grew up and into which she married. But as time went on she began to see that they were no longer productive, and in fact were causing considerable suffering. Her choices were either to stay trapped in her painful but familiar patterns, or to decide what she wanted out of life and change her old behavior and attitudes about herself and about those close to her in hopes of accomplishing something more. Here are some excerpts from her story.

The story of how Grandma Stevens had gotten me to take a bottle as a starving infant was told to me often enough for me to conclude that I owed my very life to Grandma. At least, I thought, I should try to be very much like this woman who acted selflessly, even sacrificially, and had always done "all she could" for others, the woman who saved my life. Forty years later, when I stopped being a martyr, I grieved for Annie Stevens, who no longer had anyone patterning her life after hers. The only consolation I could find was in the recognition that she had lived appropriately for her time and circumstances, and that I must do the same for mine.

When I was four years old Jane, my oldest sister, became ill with meningitis and died suddenly at the age of seven. For years Mother and my aunts talked about dear little Jane whenever they were together. Over and over I heard them say how much they had loved her and what a good, sweet girl she had been. They described her in grandiose terms: She had been the very sweetest girl in the world, she was always good, she never did anything to hurt anyone, and on and on and on. In the hope of getting some attention for myself for a change, I decided to take her place in the family. I was the oldest child, and I decided I would be the good child for them. And I would do it perfectly, always being good, never being bad or selfish or noisy or in the way. Obviously that was what they admired most.

The problem I ran into in setting out to be "good" in my family was that things were never spelled out for the children. My relatives told me that I was good, not that certain behavior or values were good. When they discussed other people, those people were always judged to be "good" or "bad." It was the person who was judged, not the person's actions. It seemed that the only way to be sure I was good was never to be bad. I spent a lot of time waiting and watching and listening for clues to acceptable behavior, and discovered one in the process. Mother started praising me to others by saying, "She's so quiet, I hardly know she's in the house." To me she said, "You're such a good girl, you would never do anything you shouldn't." She expected my two little brothers to be active, noisy, full of mischief and energy, but she seemed to think that I had some secret source of knowledge and wisdom and purity which would guide me all my life. She was never curious about my thoughts or feelings . . . she knew I was a good girl.

My father worked hard during those Depression years of the 1930s just to keep his family housed, fed, and clothed. As an electrician, he spent long hours working, earning just enough to make ends meet. He was proud of being successful in doing this during a time when many men failed to provide for their growing families. Indeed, it apparently satisfied his sense of responsibility for his children. My memories of him as a person, however, are clouded. As far as I recall, he never had much real contact with us.

There were two occasions on which I did find myself in the limelight at home during my early years. One was when report cards came out and mine would almost always be filled with all A's.

Second, I could count on close attention when my

clothes were being made. Mother sewed most of them, and Grandma sometimes helped. There were adjustments, alterations, and many opinions voiced about fit and style, and I was told repeatedly of the willingness of the seamstresses to make pretty clothes for such a good girl. Mostly, though, the boys demanded and got Mother's attention.

I did much of my serious thinking at Grandma Stevens's house. It was there that I decided, when I was about six, that Mother was right about me, that I was just naturally a quiet, good girl. It wasn't that I recognized these qualities in myself, but that I decided that if she said so, it must be so. Perhaps she knew me, even though I didn't know myself. If she were right, my future would be made up of situations over which I had no control and in which I would be helpless in many ways, self-sacrificing, and dependent on a man for support. All of these were part of being a woman to her.

My high-school years seemed typical and fairly placid, though I never felt completely sure of myself with friends who had grown up in what seemed to me to be great luxury. I did have lots of friends, however, and was known by them to be a pretty girl who did well in school. I was a loyal friend and active on the school-newspaper staff. After graduation I set off for the University of Iowa, fifty miles from my home town.

My goal at college, entirely unspoken, was to find a husband who would fit into the kind of life I had decided upon for myself. I said, of course, that I was preparing for a career. No one took that seriously enough to ask what career I had in mind with my Sociology major. I would probably have answered that since I knew of no work I would be particularly suited for, I might go on to law school. My father would have choked before he would have financed that venture for a girl. His own suggestion was that I change my major to Home Economics, where I would learn some useful skills for my life work. In fact, although I didn't tell my father, I could not even conceive of any way of life for myself that did not in-

73

clude a husband and housekeeping—although ten years later I told a friend that I thought it would be better not to educate girls at all if they were not to be allowed to use their education.

I met John Harris over a makeshift bridge table on a train crowded with students returning to Iowa City after Christmas vacation of my sophomore year, in 1948. This cocky young man quickly gave me the basic facts about himself. He was twenty-one and a senior at Iowa, majoring in Political Science. He was a track star and played clarinet in a jazz group. He planned to get a Master's degree in Business Administration and would serve two years in the Navy after graduation. He would then go to work in the family business in Davenport, which he expected to inherit eventually. One last very important fact, he said, was that he particularly liked tall brunettes.

I was so flustered by his obvious approval of me that while I explained that I was just learning to play bridge and might need some help with my bidding, I shuffled and dealt the cards in reverse order.

Our first date, the next evening, was the beginning of a stormy courtship. Part of the time I was afraid I might lose John. He was the best-looking, brightest, and most decisive man I had known, and I was tremendously impressed with him. There was no doubt that he was headed for success, and I wanted to share in it with him.

I learned to drink beer and to pet to please him, but always seemed to end up being angry with him because whatever I did was never enough. Part of the time I was afraid I would never get away from him.

I discounted my own abilities and praised his, and he agreed with me. I allowed him to make decisions for both of us, then complained about them, and he countered with criticism. He learned that he could get away with anything with me, and that my only retaliation was resentment.

Yet to our friends and families we appeared to be an extremely attractive, intelligent, carefree couple who were headed straight up the ladder of success. Our engage-

74

ment pleased my parents; they enjoyed introducing their good-looking future son-in-law to friends.

But his mother had a different reaction. She put up a persuasive argument against John's marrying me, using our young ages as a smokescreen for the real reason—she had hoped for a daughter-in-law of proper social standing. She had expected to choose a wife for John, as she had chosen and arranged every step of his and his sister's lives up to that time. Her frustration was acute when she realized that he would not let her make this decision. She finally gave in reluctantly, saying she had nothing against me personally and would be happy to have me in the family. I didn't believe her, but nevertheless I made a decision to learn to please her and keep her happy as much as possible, even at cost to myself.

During the several months we were engaged, I began to see through my own frantic role-playing. I had to admit, at least occasionally to myself, that I was disappointed that John's delight in our coming marriage was more because he had won a battle with his mother than because he was happily anticipating the time when we would live together.

I realized that I would be making a terrible mistake if I went through with our plans, but I thought that I had no choice. During spring vacation we spent one long evening at a party with friends from school. I was now drinking hard liquor; John said I had to, because "everyone" did, and I followed orders. That night when we got home, John made love to me.

From then on, I thought that if I ever wanted to marry I would have to marry John, because surely no one else would have me. Besides, I knew I would never have the nerve to tell anyone else I had done this sinful deed and that it wouldn't be fair to another man even to date him unless I confessed all. I was miserable about going ahead with plans to spend my life with John, but, believing I had no alternative, I tried to make the best of it and hoped the relationship would change after we were married.

The first few years of our marriage confirmed everything I had learned as a child to believe about myself, about men, and about life in general. I could gain my husband's approval—and having it was the only way for me to know that I was functioning properly—by being pretty to look at, especially when his friends were around, by being quiet while they studied together, and by ignoring my own duties, housework, or whatever I had planned to do, and devoting myself to his needs. I craved John's approval, but had no assurance of ever getting it.

I thought a good sex life would improve our relationship generally. But I was afraid to discuss sex openly, and didn't want to be the initiator and risk rejection, so I remained silent. John hated criticism. So we never discussed the topic.

Before long John was making sarcastic remarks or was openly critical of practically everything I did. The apartment wasn't clean enough, meals weren't served promptly or didn't appeal to him, and, worst of all, I didn't earn enough money as an office receptionist to suit him. My typical way of coping was to try even harder to please, rather than to take a realistic look at my own rights.

We had been married almost four years when our first child, Richard, was born. I was ecstatic, and hoped that having a baby would make a difference in the relationship between John and me. I did enjoy motherhood, and Richard turned out to be a particularly gifted child, though demanding. But being parents had no effect on our personal relationship. It did contribute to two major changes in our life, though. Without my salary—and we did not ever consider my going back to work after the baby was born—John worked longer and longer hours trying to get ahead in his father's firm. And we moved from our apartment to a house in a subdivision on the outskirts of town.

We both liked the neighborhood community life from the beginning. The neighbors made us welcome in many ways. We became active in the church, joined civic clubs and a bridge club, and enjoyed the status and income of professionals.

John thought it would be helpful for business contacts if I did some volunteer community work. I was asked to be a committee chairman of the League of Women Voters, I taught Sunday school, and I did volunteer work at a nearby hospital. I accepted all of these responsibilities in the hope of being helpful to my husband, though I liked what I was doing and it was gratifying to be appreciated for doing the work. John soon found that my community services interfered with my getting meals at the same time each day, and with his having my full attention. He complained, but I was not to be stopped from continuing during the next fifteen years to become a hardworking civic and church leader. However, I also learned to soften John's anger by working extra hard in our house.

John's business also flourished during those years. We eventually had three children, and our relationship with each other gradually became more aloof. The thought of ever leaving John terrified me, however, since I knew I could not support and raise three children alone.

While the younger children were pre-schoolers and Richard was in grammar school, I enjoyed my involvement with the larger community. I needed the time away from the house and children, and I loved knowing that it was possible for me to make my own contribution to my world.

At home I still couldn't do enough to please my husband. He saw me as the mother who wanted to control him and who had to be controlled in self-defense. And I recognized that, just as I had been controlled by my parents, I was continually allowing John to use and govern me in various respects. More and more I felt compelled to make an effort to change what we were doing, if possible.

And more and more I felt that the public me, outside the home, was the person I wanted to be. I knew by now that I could function well in organizations and in relation to other people, and that I enjoyed being a leader.

As the years passed I became afraid that my whole life would go by without my being able to think for myself. I spent many sleepless nights crying and telling myself that I had chosen this marriage and as a good wife I should forget the past, forgive everything, and start each day with an open mind, counting my blessings. I tortured myself for not being able or willing to do that. Once in a while John would awaken in the night and find me struggling with these thoughts, but I was never able to explain to him what I was unhappy about. He honestly believed that he was doing his duty as a husband when he provided me with the material necessities, and that he was going far beyond his duty since he gave me vacations and nice clothes.

I wanted to be treated as an equal, and to be valued as a worthwhile person. I had always paid more attention to other people's needs than to my own. I had spent many hours wishing things were different, but now a realization was beginning to dawn. Since merely wishing had never made things happen for me, I began to acknowledge what I knew to be true: Any changes in the way I would live my life would have to be initiated and seen through by me, and me in particular—not by a miraculous, spontaneous change in John, my parents, or other significant people. I had chosen my own style based on early childhood decisions which might have been inevitable at the time. I could now reassess these decisions and make new ones.

I began by examining my rights as a person. What I wanted was more respect for myself as a person of normal intelligence and capabilities, the freedom to choose my friends and to do what I pleased with them as long as my activities did not interfere with my roles as wife and mother, and for John to no longer treat me so distantly. Deep down I was afraid that he would not change enough to feel that I had these rights. I knew, too, that I would not settle for less. Whether or not we would stay together was an issue I was now willing to grapple with.

I took a long, close look at myself: forty-three years old, above-average intelligence, still reasonably good-looking, youthful in my outlook and flexible most of the time, interested in people and how they think and feel. I still had three children to raise—alone, if I eventually decided on divorce. I had no experience or education that was marketable, but I was willing to return to school to train—maybe eventually to be accepted into law school. This I wanted to do, whatever my decision about the marriage.

After I had thought this through, I registered for an assertive training class. I wanted to be comfortable with myself, to learn to relate to other people—particularly John—in ways that would give both me and them freedom and respect. And I wanted to allow myself to follow through in my decision to apply to law school—and to attend if I got accepted.

Many old beliefs have had to be changed. I've learned that I can make decisions. I want to feel I can act on them without waiting to find out if others approve or will judge my actions to be "good." I've learned it isn't necessary for me to work constantly to take care of other people; I want to feel that it's all right for me to be taken care of at times. I'm comfortable now in admitting that I'm an intelligent woman, and if that is disturbing to some man, I don't have to deny it. Now I have to learn to express opinions of my own without always needing to quote a higher authority to prove them right. I realize now that it is natural for me to be angry at times, but I want to learn to express my anger without hurting anyone else, and to know when my rights are legitimate. I want to be able to have fun without feeling guilty, and to enjoy success as much as I used to enjoy self-sacrifice.

At times changing has been a painful process. For each new way of acting or feeling or thinking, something old and familiar has had to be given up. I'm sometimes scared of the future. I think I want to continue to share my life with a man, be it John or someone else, but sometimes I am afraid that no man would want a woman who is not dependent and helpless.

Then I remember that that is one of my old beliefs and that I have chosen to reexamine old values and to rebuild a life based on what I now see as valid and true.

79

For better or worse, that is what I am doing. Changing my behavior has enabled me to be more straightforward with myself and others. I really trust myself now, and for the first time I have the strength and confidence to face my problems honestly.

If I stay with John or marry again, it will be as an equal. If I don't do either, I will still have a better life than I had when I was always losing the struggle for respect, and love. There is a time to weep and a time to laugh. I knew when I had wept enough and it was time to stop, time to change. My time to laugh and live is here.

Although the changes described here are major and farreaching, we're using this example to show a progression and a process. The process of deciding to change can apply equally well to minor matters that can be resolved in minutes rather than years.

Questionnaire:
Decision to Change

The following questions may be of value as you assess any given situation in attempting to decide whether or not to change. Add any other comments or dimensions which apply to your situation.

1. What do I gain from staying non-assertive?
   a. protection from others
   b. praise for conforming to others' expectations
   c. maintenance of a familiar behavior pattern
   d. avoidance of taking the responsibility for initiating or carrying out plans
   e. avoidance of possible conflict/anger/rejection/ acceptance of responsibility for my feelings
2. Would I be willing to give up any of the above? Which?

3. What do I lose by being non-assertive?
   a. independence
   b. the power to make decisions
   c. honesty in human relationships
   d. others' respect for my rights and wishes
   e. my ability to control my emotions (I can deny my own rights for only so long and then I blow up)
   f. relaxation, inner tranquility
   g. my ability to influence others' decisions, demands, expectations—particularly with regard to myself and what they expect me to do for or with them
   h. the satisfaction of initiating and carrying out plans
4. Do the gains of staying non-assertive outweigh the losses?
   a. If so, why?
   b. If not, am I willing to make the change by acting assertively?
   c. Can I enlist the support, understanding, and cooperation of others involved either in the situation or in my life?
5. What are my short-term goals? (in my relationships and in my activities).
6. What are my long-term goals?
7. How can assertive behavior help me achieve these goals?

5

Clues to Assertive Problems— Are You Chewing Your Pencil?

SEVEN twenty-five A.M. Marcia wakes up her three children and hurries them through the before-school routine. Jimmy, seven, leaves his pajamas on the floor as he gets dressed in front of the T.V. Jody, twelve, arrives at the breakfast table two minutes before he has to leave for school and picks a fight with Monica, ten. Marcia frowns but says nothing.

Her husband, Ben, comes into the kitchen, whistling as he gets ready to leave for work, and tells Marcia that he may bring a business associate home for dinner, even though he knows she'll be racing out at 7:45 P.M. to go to a class. She reluctantly agrees, hoping he'll notice her lack of enthusiasm. Everyone finally leaves, and Marcia prepares to clean up the ravages of the morning's activities.

Then something happens. It doesn't happen suddenly, and Marcia can't put her finger on it, but soon a morning headache is coming on. She takes an aspirin and starts to do the seemingly endless household chores. She gives up temporarily, sits down, and eats a big piece of strawberry shortcake left over from last night's dinner, even though she's not really hungry.

As she eats she hears the neighbors' dog in her garden, and when she looks out she sees a trail of broken tomato plants. She'd like to call up her neighbor and tell her about the dog, but something seems to be holding her back. And by the time she turns around, her children are chattering noisily as they return home for lunch. Marcia snaps at them.

What's happening?

She doesn't know. She can point to lots of little things that bother her somewhat, but she can't see why they add up to something big, something which she can't quite identify, except to complain to Betty, her sister, who is visiting for the afternoon, that things just aren't right.

When Marcia described her situation to the assertive training group that evening, she said, "I've spent most of my life helping other people, first as the oldest child in a family of four, and for a long time now with my own family. I've always played the role of peacemaker and tried to smooth over other people's conflicts, and to avoid conflicts myself.

"But lately I'm starting to get tired of trying to please everyone else. I'd like to be able to do something just for myself. Sometimes I'm not even sure what that is, except to have some peace and quiet, though I do know I'd like to get rid of these head aches, have more energy—and lose about fifteen pounds.

"At other times, when I finally realize what I do want, it's either too late to do anything or I'm so frustrated or angry that I don't dare open my mouth for fear that I'll explode. Of course, sometimes I do blow up—and take it out on the children, especially— but it's not worth it because I feel so guilty afterward.

"What I want to know," she concluded, "is how I can learn to be *aware* of what I'm feeling or what I want—and how to express myself appropriately."

The group discussed ways in which Marcia could increase her own awareness. They agreed that often *if we simply think about the circumstances, we will be able to identify the problem.* "The dog is ruining my garden." "Jimmy messes up the house in the morning." "Jody should be on time for breakfast." "Having dinner guests when I've got to rush off right after the meal is too complicated." Once we recognize the problem, we can *establish goals, think of alternative ways to accomplish them, weigh the alternatives, and act*—on the most likely, or desired, or least threatening, or whatever seems the most suitable, option.

In other cases, if our problem is more difficult to identify, we may want to begin by *examining the clues that our own bodies or behavior provide*—such as anxiety, aggression, procrastination, feeling "low" or "blue," or playing games. Being *aware of the clues* may help us identify the problem. "I know when I get a headache in the morning even after a good night's sleep, or when I eat when I'm not hungry, that something's wrong. Maybe when that happens I should just stop and look around at my life and say, 'What's bothering me?'" Again, once the problem is identified, then the process of solving it is the same as before: Determine the goals, consider alternative solutions, weigh them, and decide how to assert ourselves in order to accomplish them.

In this chapter we will talk about the various recognizable cues that we get from our own bodies and behavior patterns. Once we realize *what these cues and patterns are and how they work,* we should be better able to *recognize situations in which we're having trouble being assertive.* Then we can begin to pinpoint what and when we want to change.

Body Cues: Manifestations of Anxiety

Anxiety inhibits assertive behavior. So, feeling anxious, tense, or apprehensive is often our signal to ourselves that we are failing to be assertive. We may be generally uneasy, or worried about what may happen in the near or more remote future. Sometimes our anxiety shows up in nervous behavior like trembling, nail biting, teeth grinding, finger tapping, foot jiggling, and joyless laughter. We may develop insomnia, or loss—or exaggeration—of appetite. These cues, although not invariably associated with anxiety, may be present before, during, or after situations which require assertive behavior.

Obviously, not all anxiety is related to non-assertive behavior, but when we are trying to heighten our awareness about our own needs for assertion, we should pay particular attention to the symptoms of anxiety. Very often we will find some underlying situation with which we can cope by being assertive.

Sometimes physical symptoms of anxiety are clearly related to assertion. Kathleen described the sensations she feels when she's sitting in class and wants to ask the teacher a question: "I know there's no rational reason to be nervous. But even when I recognize exactly what I want to ask, I can feel the anxiety building up inside me. At other times I feel the physical anxiety before I'm even aware that I want to say something. In either case, my heart starts racing and my throat tightens up. Most of the time I just sit there and don't say anything. When the teacher goes on to another topic, I'm relieved and can feel my body relax. But later I'm angry with myself because I haven't spoken up and found out what I needed to know."

Kathleen knows that her anxiety is related to her fear of asking questions in class. She knows what she wants to do—to work on speaking out in class, and to overcome the obstacles to her assertion.

At other times we experience the tension associated with our anxiety but we're not sure why we're anxious. When this happens, when our bodies give us cues that say "Pay attention to me," it may be helpful to examine what is going on in our lives or relationships that might be making us anxious. Instead of trying to avoid anxiety by ignoring it, taking a tranquilizer, or keeping very busy with other matters, we may want to explore what the problem is and recognize what we want.

Janet, a serious woman who had complained of general feelings of tension without being able to pinpoint them, told us that after we had asked her to become aware of her body's cues to anxiety she had gone home and kept a journal in chart form (see page 96 at end of chapter) for a week. Daily she recorded the specific situations in which she felt anxious, her particular feelings of tension, and their physical manifestations. Through keeping the journal, she realized that she tightened her jaws whenever she became anxious, which she did whenever she had to deny requests. As a secretary in a busy office, she was constantly juggling demands from her bosses and their clients, and often had to refuse requests for appointments and services.

"It's amazing," she said later. "I had never realized how frequently my jaw tenses. If I'd known about this years ago I could have saved a lot of money in dental bills. Some of my teeth have been capped because of the constant tension. At least I know now what to work on—I've got to do something about asserting myself and saying *no* to people without taking it out on my poor teeth."

Certainly not all situations are as dramatic as Janet's. However, even the slightest of cues can help us to become aware of our own feelings, so we must look to our bodies for the cues to our own anxieties. Although our reactions may be varied, most of us can identify one or two characteristic cues then pay more careful attention to them when they occur.

Behavior Patterns: Avoiding Assertiveness

The behavior patterns we will discuss now can also be cues that we are not handling a situation assertively.

Lashing Out: Aggressive

Sometimes when we are faced with a situation that makes us anxious, we literally clench our fists, inhale sharply—and blurt out our angry reactions. This kind of aggressive outburst may indicate that in this particular situation assertion is difficult for us. When we are non-assertive we submit to our anxiety; when we are aggressive we may well be avoiding our anxiety and avoiding assertion itself, since the very act of an angry, aggressive outburst, designed to put someone down, temporarily alleviates our anxiety. But the results are often destructive. At times we have to decide whether or not the short-range satisfaction of blowing up is worth the long-range price of damaged relationships, or the time and effort it will take to repair them later.

For example, Ann described her pattern of aggressive outbursts toward her roommate, Libby, who had moved into Ann's apartment on the understanding that the arrangement would be for only a few weeks. Six months later Libby was still there, with no signs of leaving. In fact, her records crammed Ann's bookshelf, her wet laundry overflowed the tiny bathroom, her ivy climbed the walls—and so did Ann.

Ann grew more and more hostile toward Libby. She blew up at her for leaving dishes in the sink, for adopting a kitten, and for having guests over for dinner. The usually even-tempered Ann often felt out of control, and was disturbed by her repeated aggression toward Libby. After talking with the group about this, Ann began to realize that each time her tension built up she had attacked Libby for minor annoyances. Nevertheless, she had avoided asserting herself on the major issue—the fact that she wanted Libby to move out.

Examining her pattern of aggressive behavior helped Ann focus on the nature of her relationship with Libby. She had intensified her anger to the point where she was eager to kick Libby out, and to tell her off in the process. Ann acknowledged that one gigantic aggressive outburst about Libby's prolonged stay might temporarily relieve her tension, and would probably get Libby out.

Yet when Ann looked at the overall situation she decided that the goal was to have Libby leave the apartment, but on friendly terms. So Ann decided to try to handle the situation assertively rather than aggressively: She would simply ask Libby to move out within two weeks, and would stick to her decision firmly but without any angry attacks.

Before she decided to assert herself directly, Ann

had been misdirecting her angry feelings, shifting them to inconsequential side issues. Her misplaced anger had been ineffective. She hadn't told Libby that what she really wanted was to have her move out. In spite of her repeated outbursts, she had been left with her own frustration about the situation, and, even worse, she felt guilty about her aggressive outbursts—until she made her decision to confront Libby honestly and directly.

It is common to swing from one extreme to another, from non-assertive to aggressive behavior. We may repress our feelings or ideas until they erupt in an aggressive outburst. In building our awareness, it is useful to examine our own patterns of aggressive behavior or sudden outbursts. Sometimes we may inappropriately lash out at someone without confronting the real source of our anger. At other times we may misdirect our anger, or lash out at a person other than the one at whom we are angry. In situations such as these our aggressive outbursts may be a cue to the fact that we are avoiding assertive behavior.

Procrastination

Before making a decision it is important to gather and weigh information, so a certain amount of indecisiveness may be appropriate. But once we have made a decision to do something but put off actually doing it, we may be avoiding assertion. For instance, Jennifer, a laboratory technician, knew that her director, Dr. Strand, was hiring additional people to work on an interesting new research project. Jennifer wanted to give up her current position and work with the new team, but she never seemed to find the right moment to mention it to Dr. Strand. If she continued to procrastinate long enough, the director would have hired all the necessary people, and Jennifer could then rationalize that it was "too late anyway."

Jennifer discussed her anxiety over asking Dr. Strand about the new job: "I guess I've been putting it off because I'm afraid that Dr. Strand will get angry and think I've got a lot of nerve trying to push myself into the project. Maybe I'm hoping she'll ask me if I want to work with the new team before I have to ask her."

If Jennifer continues to be silent, ultimately other people's decisions will take over for her. This is *totally* non-assertive behavior, in which Jennifer is giving up any control over the situation.

Procrastination is not always related to non-assertion. Faithful Penelope procrastinated for ten years before choosing a suitor to succeed Odysseus, but that was an intentional stalling technique, since she had kept hoping that he would eventually come home. Yet many procrastinations are non-assertive, and it is useful to ask ourselves, when we recognize that we are putting matters off and putting them off: "Am I procrastinating now because I'm reluctant to assert myself?"

The following questions are useful indicators of procrastination:

1. Do I put off making or returning phone calls?
2. Do I delay accepting or refusing invitations?
3. Do I delay asking for needed information?
4. Do I put off confronting people?
5. Do I postpone telling others my feelings or opinions, even though I know what I want to say?

6. Do I delay asking for help even though I want it?

Yes answers may help us to identify situations in which we procrastinate because of difficulty in asserting ourselves.

Delayed Reaction

Sometimes we get our cues after the fact. For instance, we may find ourselves thinking, after we have said or done something we wish we hadn't, "Why didn't I say what I was actually thinking?" "Why did I agree to do that? I didn't really want to." This sort of mulling over a situation after it is done is a cue to us that we have failed to take an assertive stance. It may be too late to change that particular situation, but being aware of our reaction and making a mental note of it may help avoid repeating it in the future.

After we discussed this with an assertive training group, Marian became very animated and said, "Oh, that's me! Every time someone invites me anywhere, whether it's a social event or a meeting or a movie, I find myself saying, 'Sure, I'll do it,' even if I have no interest in it, or shouldn't take the time to go. Later I could kick myself for getting so overcommitted."

Gail, another group member, replied, "I know what you mean. I do the same thing, and then I'm resentful that the other person asked me."

Marian agreed and said, "I don't want to hurt other people's feelings, but I don't like being hassled by trying to do everything I've said I'll do."

"All right," the group leader pointed out, "you recognize the problem. You see the pattern that you're in—all those times that you ask yourselves after the fact, 'Why did I say *yes*?' 'Why did I let that happen?' Now, what are you going to do about it?"

Marian thought for a minute and said, "Well, when I feel stuck or I'm not sure what I want to do, I could just say, 'Thanks. I appreciate your asking me, but I tend to get involved in more than I can handle. Let me think it over and let you know tomorrow.' Then I'd have some breathing space, time to figure out what I really want to do."

It was important for Marian and Gail to learn to recognize times when they were genuinely reluctant to make on-the-spot decisions. They could reexamine their typical behavior and determine which sorts of decisions they would actually feel best about making on the spot, and which ones they needed to have time to think over before making up their minds. Putting off a decision until we're certain—or more nearly certain—of the most preferable alternative can eliminate the resentments we feel after having made decisions that are wrong for us, decisions made in response to our inner pressure to avoid conflict.

Asking for delay of this sort is not putting off assertive action; it reflects a conscious decision to give ourselves some *limited* extra time to make a decision with which we are going to feel comfortable. The request for such a delay is in fact an assertion for time out—time to think.

Feeling "Low"

In our society women are permitted, if not expected, to feel "blue," to have "the blahs," to be mildly depressed—states of mind and body sufficiently common for Sigmund Freud to consider "normal." We are not talking here about long-lasting states of severe depression, but rather the slightly-letdown feeling, which is often accompanied by lack of enthusiasm and energy, and which we usually can't find any particular reason for. One explanation for this letdown feeling is that by failing to assert ourselves in situations in which we would like to do so, we are letting frustration and anger build up and then turning them inward. So instead of expressing ourselves openly and outwardly, the "blues," our interior monologue of gloom, becomes the psychological price we pay for our non-assertive behavior.

Lisa, a waitress at a pizza restaurant, told us that she had come home from work every night feeling generally down and mildly depressed. After discussing this with the assertive training group, she realized that she resented having to wipe off all the tables at closing time while Teresa, her co-worker, had only to fill the ketchup bottles, an easier and quicker task. She decided to ask Teresa to share the chores equally, and reported the next week that she really did feel better each night at closing time.

Although the issue may seem trivial, the fact was that it *did* bother Lisa, and it continued to do so until with a simple request she did something to relieve her depression.

Holiday times are particularly likely to produce such feelings of low-level tension, and they are all the more painful because of the external pressures toward gaiety and exuberance. Nora's situation, as she explained it to our assertive training group the week before Thanksgiving, is typical.

"You know how it is at this time of year," said Nora, an energetic woman in her fifties, who had become quite well-known in the city as a result of her weekly radio program. "You can't open a newspaper or magazine without seeing recipes for holiday food. Wherever I turn there are reminders of the holiday season coming up—in the stores, on the TV and radio, decorations on the streets, ads in the mail. And the more frantic their encouragements to festivity become, the more out of it I feel, just blah. I can't work up my usual enthusiasm for the season—the shopping, the entertaining, let alone writing Christmas cards and preparing the house for the return of my kids with their families and friends. I guess my 'low' came across when I talked with my daughter on the phone last night. She kept asking me what was bugging me, but I just couldn't put my finger on it.

"After I hung up I started thinking about her reaction to me—and about the way I was feeling. Since assertive training has been on my mind a lot lately, I started asking myself, 'What am I really feeling? What do I really want?' What I realized is that I'm not just feeling down or depressed. I'm really feeling resentful toward the rest of the family for always putting the burden on me to prepare and hostess all the holiday celebrations. Thanksgiving is just the beginning; the entertaining goes on through Christmas and New Year's—and it's always at my house. Sure, other people help out—my husband and the kids get the Christmas tree and decorate it, for instance—but guess who takes it down.

"The main responsibility falls on me. It will again this year, I know, because it always has. And I guess that's why I always end up feeling glum and slightly depressed at this time of the year—I know I'm going to have a lot of extra work, and a lot of organizing, too. But then I feel guilty about not having the proper spirit—and I certainly wouldn't want to say anything about how I feel and spoil the holidays for everyone else."

"Well," said another woman, "now that you realize why you're low during the holidays, what are you going to do about it? It's not enough just to say, 'Aha, that's why I'm blue.'"

"I don't know," said Nora. "I've always done most of the holiday shopping and cooking and baking and cleaning . . . and my family counts on it. I could take extra naps, to have more energy. Or I could take some tranquilizers."

"Those are just ways to help you put up with what you don't like," scoffed a group member about the age of Nora's daughter. "They're not a solution. Did it ever occur to you that all the time you're saying, 'The responsibility *falls* on me,' you're really *accepting* the responsibility? Don't you think that your family has come to expect you to run the whole show during the holidays because *you've* always expected to do it and have always done it?"

"Well, I guess so."

"Then how could you be assertive about making a change in your family's holiday pattern?"

Nora thought for a bit. "I could simply ask them all for more help. Knowing my family, it wouldn't do just to make a general announcement—I'd have to suggest specific tasks for each person. And I could parcel out some of the big family dinners, too. They don't always have to be at our home!" Her enthusiasm increased. "Since we're all having Thanksgiving at our house, as usual, I'll bring it up over dinner that day."

"No!" another member fairly shouted out.

Nora looked startled. "Why not?"

"The timing's wrong! It would work better if you could get everybody together before the holiday, when they're in a good mood and feeling relaxed and cooperative. Then they won't think you're laying a guilt trip on them by coming on like a martyr during the dinner. That could ruin the dinner and make the rest of the family resentful too."

"You're right." Nora looked pleased. "I'll do it Sunday afternoon this weekend, when we're together. That's usually a good time for discussions. We could set family policy for holiday times in general."

And that's what they did. Nora was amazed to find out that the family was actually delighted to share the responsibilities. Christmas dinner was planned that afternoon and Nora was to bring the dessert to her daughter's house!

In situations such as Lisa's and Nora's, as in many others, our negative feelings may be a cue, a plea for us to pay attention to ourselves. In so doing, we may be able to decide why we're depressed. Once we recognize the causes, we can begin to figure out what we want to express, and then start to do something about it.

Checklist:
When I May Be Acting Non-Assertively

This checklist is a shortcut to recognizing behavioral cues that may signal the need for assertive behavior. Recognizing these symptoms can help us identify situations which we may want to write up and analyze in the journal which follows the checklist.

A. Am I aware when and if I have any of these symptoms, and whether these are related to anxiety?

96

1. teeth grinding
2. nail biting
3. finger or foot tapping
4. foot jiggling
5. artificial, nervous laughter
6. insomnia
7. stomach churning
8. heart beating fast
9. jaw tightening
10. headache
11. tight neck muscles
12. other personal ways of expressing tensions

B. Do I do any of the following things to avoid assertion?

1. lash out, have aggressive outbursts
2. procrastinate
3. repress my feelings
4. feel "low"
5. give in to please others

Journal
It's Important to Keep One

Even though it requires some effort, keeping a journal in chart form is one of the most important things we can do for ourselves. It helps us pinpoint the specific situations in which we want to work to behave more assertively. We suggest that you keep such a chart for at least a week so that you can analyze your behavior patterns. The chart will be a big help when we get to Chapter Eleven, "Putting It All Together—Building Assertive Skills." And when we reach the point of systematically practicing our assertive skills (don't give up, we will), if you have kept a journal it will be much easier for you to go right to work on the situations which are difficult for you to handle assertively.

One Woman's Journal

Situation and date.	Physical symptoms, body cues and behavior patterns.	My behavior.	How I felt.	What I would like to have done.	Why I didn't do what I wanted to.
Thu. 2/23 Teacher kept talking over my head. Wanted to ask a question.	Heart beating fast.	Kept quiet.	Ignorant and frustrated.	Asked my question.	Afraid of appearing ignorant.
Sat. 2/25 Friends dropped in at dinner time.	Jaw tightens, voice tenses.	Invited them to stay and eat with us.	Trapped and angry. Worried that there wasn't enough to eat and that the tablecloth looked messy.	Explained that I had dinner ready for Jim and myself and asked them to leave.	Felt I'd offend them.
My husband called me at my office and asked me to meet him after work to go out to dinner and a movie	Biting my lip, tapping pencil while talking to him.	I agreed to meet him, rather reluctantly, hoping he'd hear the hesitation in my voice.	Resentful that he didn't realize how tired I was.	Told him that I didn't want to go this evening and that I had really been looking forward to relaxing together at home.	I was afraid I'd hurt his feelings and spoil his plans.

6

What's the Worst that Could Happen?—
Irrational Beliefs

"**I**F I say I don't want to go to the hockey game, they'll get mad." *Irrational belief*.

"What right have I to question the mechanic's judgment—and bill? He knows more about cars than I do." *Irrational belief*.

"If I don't listen to my neighbor's problems every time she drops in unannounced, she won't like me and I'll feel awful." *Irrational belief*.

"It's wrong for me to refuse to collect for such a worthy charity." *Irrational belief*.

"If we don't spend every Sunday with my mother-in-law she'll be terribly hurt, and it will be our fault." *Irrational belief*.

If assertive behavior is merely the direct and appropriate expression of our ideas, needs, or feelings—and every woman's right and obligation to herself—then why should assertiveness be such a problem? In reality, many of us are inhibited, afraid to behave as assertively as we would like. This is partly because we have so many anxieties about the supposedly negative effects of being direct.

These anxieties stem from irrational beliefs, a concept developed by Dr. Albert Ellis, founder of rational emotive therapy. Irrational beliefs distort reality by focusing on and anticipating the "disastrous," "awful," "worst possible" outcomes of assertive behavior. When we subscribe to these irrational beliefs, we are overly concerned with how we think others will react. We usually end up deferring to them. Irrational beliefs are not based on reality but rather on nightmarish fantasy —we imagine the most negative possible results of acting assertively. Our thinking is irrational when we focus on these negative fantasies and ignore all the positive possibilities that might result from our assertiveness. Whether or not we have picked these beliefs up from our parents, or our culture, they prevail by inhibiting many of us today.

For the purposes of assertive training, we and others have adapted Ellis's basic premise that "Several powerful, irrational and illogical ideas stand in the way of our leading anxiety-free, unhostile lives."[6] Ellis believes that we can change our emotions or our feelings about ourselves by changing these irrational beliefs and replacing them with rational ones. This way we can reduce the anxiety that inhibits assertive behavior and become more likely to act in an appropriate, assertive manner.

When we apply Ellis's premise to the development of assertive behavior, we begin by trying to pinpoint our particular irrational beliefs and then replacing them with new, rational beliefs. Rational beliefs are based on a realistic assessment of a given situation and the recognition that there is not just one but many possible outcomes of any particular assertive action. Furthermore, it is rational to believe that even if the result of our assertion is negative, we can handle the resulting defeat, for we can choose not to be devastated by it.

Once we have recognized our irrational beliefs and have tried to replace them with rational ones, we can then begin to *act* on the basis of these new beliefs. It is a good idea to make our first attempts at assertion in situations that we can handle fairly easily, with a low level of risk, and in which we are likely to succeed. Eventually we can work up to more complicated situations, with higher stakes. Each time we behave assertively and get positive reinforcement, we become less anxious and more likely to try being assertive again. As Joseph Wolpe has emphasized, "What is needed is activity. To understand that you have it in you [to cause changes] doesn't change anything. It is the action. . . . Every time that you behave so as to express non-anxious emotion and the action is successful, you are doing something to build up a habit."[7] Assertive behavior really replaces bad old habits with good new ones.

Irrational Belief #1
If I assert myself, others will get mad at me.

Rational counterparts to #1
If I assert myself, the effects may be positive, neutral, or negative. However, since assertion involves legitimate rights, I feel that the odds are in my favor to have some positive result.

Possible applications of this are: *If I assert myself people may or may not get mad at me/they may feel closer to me/like what I say or do/help me to solve the problem.*

Irrational Belief #2
If I assert myself and people do become angry with me, I will be devastated: it will be awful.

102

Rational Counterparts to #2

a. *Even if others do become angry and unpleasant, I am capable of handling it without falling apart.*

b. *If I assert myself when it is appropriate, I don't have to feel responsible for the other person's anger. It may be his problem.*

Both these irrational beliefs can make us anxious and can keep us from behaving assertively. If we have learned, as many of us have, that conflict is terrible, that it's better to placate than to aggravate, we may tell ourselves that to risk evoking anger in someone else is potentially too threatening to attempt. Our "peace at any price" attitude may make us the Neville Chamberlains of our own worlds. We may be sending ourselves subconscious messages such as "If someone gets very mad at me, I won't be able to handle it. I'll feel horrible. I'll cry." Or "If someone blows up at me I'll explode back and lose control. That would be awful."

These irrational beliefs influenced Sara, a young married woman with two small children, who explained her situation to one of our assertive training groups. She was afraid of speaking out and starting an argument with Harry, her father-in-law, who customarily stopped at her house two or three times a week to visit his grandchildren on his way home from work. He would appear just at "tension time"—when the children were tired, the house was messy, and Sara was feeling most pressured to prepare dinner and maintain some order in her universe.

As Sara described this scene, her voice grew strained and her face showed considerable tension. She said, "I don't really mind that Dad visits at this hour. As a matter of fact, it might be nice to have him come in and play with the kids for a while at five o'clock. But whenever he comes, he makes sarcastic remarks like 'Oh, I guess you've been too busy with your social schedule to notice the chocolate pudding splattered on the wall here.' Or 'These kids are lovely, dear, but you wouldn't be using up the city's water supply if you gave them a bath once in a while.' I feel so angry when he says something like that, I could scream!"

But Sara doesn't scream. She merely withdraws and nods at him with a weak smile, or occasionally murmurs softly, "That's not funny."

When we asked Sara how she felt about this situation, she replied, "Anxious, nervous, boiling inside. Every time I see him walking up the path to our house my stomach starts churning. However," she added, "he *is* rather caustic, and I'm so afraid if I tell him that I want him to stop making critical remarks if he wants to continue to drop over, well, I'm afraid he'll blow up at me and give me that old line about being immature and having no sense of humor. Why, if he started to yell at me, I'd probably just stand there and cry. I wouldn't know what to do."

As Sara decided to work on ways to confront Harry, we asked her to start by examining some of her irrational beliefs and other options. She had assumed that Harry's response, even to a calm, direct statement of the problem, would be anger. She had imagined the worst, focused on it, and irrationally blocked out all other possible reactions. Now she was ready to take a look at some alternatives.

"Well," she finally said, "I guess he might not get mad. He might just say, 'Hey, why didn't you tell me that before? I didn't know my little jokes bothered you.' Or maybe, 'Oh, come on, Sara. You know I love you!' Of course, then I'd have to stress again, even more emphatically, that I really do want him to stop his cutting remarks. There are many ways he could answer, and it would be irrational to expect only the worst response. I guess I'll never find out exactly how he'll react unless I talk to him."

It is possible that if Sara asserts herself in a caring yet direct way she and Harry will resolve this difficulty, for she is making a negotiable demand in a potentially workable situation.

But what if Harry does become angry? That is, of course, one possibility. How could Sara deal with his anger? We discussed the matter with Sara at length, and agreed that being the recipient of another's anger is unpleasant but need not be devastating.

Sara finally said, "Well, O.K. I don't like to have people angry at me. But I feel terrible about this situation the way it is now. If Dad gets angry—and he may or may not—*I don't have to feel responsible for his anger*. He's the one who is choosing to get mad. And I won't shrivel up and die if he does. I don't *have* to be so vulnerable to others' moods. Just because he's angry at me doesn't make me an awful person. And it doesn't mean he'll stay offended forever."

Then Sara shook her head and exclaimed, "Wow! That makes so much sense. But I've done everything I could to avoid conflict all my life, because I've been afraid that it would be too hard to handle. I don't think I can change that overnight."

We agreed that Sara wouldn't change dramatically overnight, that her new insight was not some magic potion which would immediately transform her into an assertive woman with no anxiety about anger. Since many of us have already overlearned non-assertive habits by having repeated the behavior hundreds or thousands of times, it is reasonable to expect that behaving assertively will require considerable attention and practice before becoming as familiar, even as comfortable, as the old behavior used to be.

The realization that the logical consequence of her assertive behavior was not necessarily anger helped Sara reduce her apprehension about dealing directly with Harry. And her expanded horizons allowed for some satisfactory possibilities in their relationship, instead of only the two devastating alternatives she had previously imagined: bottling it up or having it out. We encouraged Sara to repeat her rational beliefs to herself often, thus reducing her anxiety about confronting Harry and making it easier to try out her assertive behavior.

After Sara had practiced in the group what she intended to say to Harry and had received constructive commentary from the leaders and group members, she observed, "That felt good. This week I'm going to tell Dad what I've been wanting to say for the past year. Even if he does get mad, we can probably work it out."

Sara later told us that she and her husband had invited Harry over for dinner one evening after the children were in bed. When the dinner was over and everyone was relaxed, she calmly (although her heart was pounding) told Harry that, much as she appreciated his interest in the children, it made her angry when he made sarcastic remarks about her care of them and her housekeeping. Then she asked if he'd stop.

Much to her relief, Harry wasn't angry at all—only surprised because he hadn't realized that he had been upsetting her. He promised to stop, and "He's kept his promise, said Sara, "and the tension between us has evaporated."

Irrational Belief #3
Although I prefer others to be straightforward with me, I'm afraid that if I am open with others and say 'no,' I will hurt them.

Rational Counterparts to #3
a. *If I'm assertive, other people may or may not feel hurt.*
b. *Most people are not more fragile than I am. If I prefer to be dealt with directly, quite likely others will too.*

Irrational Belief #4
If my assertion hurts others, I am responsible for their feelings.

Rational Counterparts to #4
a. *Even if others do feel hurt by my assertive behavior, I can let them know I care for them while also being direct about what I need or want.*
b. *Although at times others will be taken aback by my assertive behavior, most people are not so vulnerable and fragile that they will be shattered by it.*

Pat, a woman of about fifty who was usually rather quiet in the group, suddenly spoke: "O.K. I can see how it's possible to handle conflict or anger, even if we don't like it, though I now realize I was brought up to avoid it. But what most often keeps me from asserting myself is my fear that if I do, I'll hurt someone else's feelings. I'm sensitive about the way people

107

treat me, and I'm sensitive about how I treat other people. I hate to hurt other people's feelings.

"I'm faced with a situation right now," she went on, "that may not seem important, but it bothers me a lot. My husband and I are going to Chicago for a convention in three weeks. Whenever we're there we stay with my sister Hazel, and I know she really enjoys our visits. But even though John and I usually like to be with Hazel, on this trip we want to stay in a hotel and have some time just to ourselves. We haven't had a vacation for two years, and the idea of spending five days by ourselves in the city sounds great to us both. But I don't know how to tell Hazel. I'm so afraid she'll be hurt. I'd feel terrible if I thought I'd made her feel bad."

Pat's comments are based on the irrational belief that assertive behavior with even the slightest negative overtones will hurt others' feelings. A similar belief is that if the other person's feelings are hurt as a result of our assertiveness, we are responsible. We may exaggerate this belief to include the possibility that not only have we hurt the other person's feelings, but she'll probably never recover from the blow, and our relationship with her will be ruined forever—irrationalities due perhaps more to anxiety over our right to honest expression than actual experiences of offending people.

When we confronted Pat with the irrational belief that was keeping her from asserting herself, especially when we exaggerated this belief to the point of absurdity, Pat responded, "Yes, I guess I'm assuming that Hazel will be terribly upset if we don't stay with her. But after our discussion I have to admit that I don't know whether she will be or not. In fact, it's possible that she might prefer not to cook and clean for us for five days; she might think we'd all have a better time if we planned some activities together but didn't stay together.

"And even if her feelings are hurt," Pat continued, "we can talk it over. After all, we really do care about each other. Our relationship can survive a minor disappointment."

Pat had begun to replace her irrational focus on only one possible outcome of her assertion with other reactions Hazel might have. It is not realistic to believe people are so vulnerable that if we assert ourselves they will fall apart. Our own experiences contradict that. Nor is it rational to assume that our relationships with people are so fragile that they can't survive some ups and downs.

When we asked Pat how she would have wanted the out-of-towners to act if she were in Hazel's position, she replied, "Why, of course I'd understand if a couple wanted to be alone. I might feel disappointed but I'd feel even worse if I thought they had stayed with me just out of a sense of obligation." The other group members agreed that they too would rather be told the truth even if they were displeased by it, for in the long run it is easier to cope with the known than with the unknown, with the direct and honest rather than with that which is covert or manipulative.

Of course there are exceptions to this, and there are times when we may not choose to be direct. For instance, in the interests of family harmony we may choose to overlook the irritating behavior of a relative we seldom see, on those rare occasions when we do see her. We may ignore the rudeness of a bus driver if we're in a hurry to get somewhere. Or we may put up with a nagging boss if the price of an assertion is the loss of a job.

Yet in other circumstances, perhaps in long-term relationships, where there is time to explore the subtleties and work out difficulties, people who refuse to behave assertively can often cause more problems than they avoid. Their hesitancy, self-effacing behavior, or sending of double messages can be extraordinarily frustrating to people trying to deal with them. If we don't receive a clear message, we can't respond with a clear answer; we don't know how to behave.

So Lucy, another group member, fumed: "It takes so much energy to get a straight answer out of my mother. Whenever I ask if she would like to babysit for the kids she answers, with an audible sigh and a noticeable lack of enthusiasm, 'Anything you like, dear.' So I keep on asking her, 'But do you *really want to?*' But instead of telling me directly what she wants she keeps sending me those double messages— 'I do and I don't want to babysit.' I'd feel so much more comfortable if I knew where I stood—even if it meant she never took care of my children."

Over and over in the assertive training groups women say that they prefer others to be direct with them. We point out that it is unnecessary to operate on a behavioral double standard—to think that while we ourselves like the straightforward dealings of others, everyone else is so vulnerable that we have to protect them by being non-assertive. By behaving openly and directly ourselves, we can relieve ourselves of the burden of "taking care" of others' supposed— but perhaps nonexistent—vulnerabilities. Assertiveness can generate reciprocal assertiveness, and thus can help to build open and honest relationships.

110

Irrational Belief #5

It is wrong and selfish to turn down legitimate requests. Other people will think I'm terrible and won't like me.

Rational Counterparts to #5

a. *Even legitimate requests can be refused assertively.*
b. *It is acceptable to consider my own needs—sometimes before those of others.*
c. *I can't please all of the people all of the time.*

It is hard to refuse requests, partly because of the common irrational belief that it is wrong and selfish to turn down legitimate requests. The more justifiable something seems to us ("You've *got* to help me. You're the *only one* who can do this."), the more afraid we may be to deny it. We may be torn between what we ourselves want and what we feel we should do to keep the other person's affection.

In such circumstances we may often find ourselves doing things we don't want to do, being with people we would rather not be with, spending our time the way someone else wants us to spend it, rather than choosing for ourselves. We may tell ourselves, "I can't possibly turn down a valid request or say *no*." "I don't want to be selfish." "If I don't do favors for others I won't be able to ask them to do favors for me." "If I don't do what other people want, they won't like me. Wouldn't that be awful? I'd lose their friendship [or love]." Some of these concerns may influence whether or not we say *no* to men who want sex more than we do—particularly if we care for them and want to keep seeing them.

Ellen has a problem. Her friend Jeanne is running

111

for city council and has asked Ellen to hostess a series of coffees for her in Ellen's home. Ellen told us, "I don't have any legitimate reason why I can't do it. I like Jeanne and want her to win the election, but I just don't want to put the time and energy she's asked for into this campaign. But how can I say *no*? She's my friend. I don't want her to think that I don't like her, or that I'm just a selfish, uncaring person. I certainly don't want to lose her friendship."

Ellen is getting nervous because she's focusing, irrationally, *only* on the possible negative reactions that Jeanne might have. She hasn't even considered the possibility that Jeanne might appreciate her honesty, and that she might respect Ellen's right to her own reasons.

Ellen unrealistically believes that it is unacceptable to consider her own wishes, at times before those of others, especially if others have good reasons for their demands. She is doing Jeanne a disservice by irrationally believing Jeanne to be so self-centered that her good will depends on Ellen's willingness to help her out whenever she asks. And Ellen does their friendship a disservice, by irrationally assuming it so fragile that a single *no* would destroy it.

Certainly we realize that not everyone can be pleased with us all the time. To try always to accommodate everybody, our personalities would have to deteriorate to amoebalike blobs, neither attractive nor recognizable from one moment to the next. And who would we be?

Ellen discussed the situation at length with her assertive training group, and eventually chose to replace her customary irrational beliefs with some rational ones. She decided to assert herself with Jeanne. The next week she reported, matter-of-factly, that she had told Jeanne she wouldn't hostess all the coffees, but would handle one as a favor to a friend. She explained, "I simply called up Jeanne and said, 'I'm glad you're running for councilwoman. I support you all the way, but I really don't want to hostess all the coffees for you. I'll do one, if you like.'

"By the time I got the words out, my voice was starting to quiver, but did I ever feel good when she responded, 'Well, I'm glad you're hostessing one, though it would be a big help if you could do more. Just the same, I understand and, believe me, every bit of help counts. We all have to set our own priorities, and I guess politics isn't your bag.' "

As the other members of the group praised Ellen's success, one asked, "But what would you have done if she had sounded hurt or angry?"

Ellen responded, "I had made up my mind before I called that even if she were hurt it wouldn't be the end of our friendship. Also, I told myself that I just can't keep everyone else happy at my expense. I decided that if she sounded hurt or angry, I'd make it as clear as possible that I cared about her, but that I was making a choice to turn down her request. And I had included what for me was a workable compromise—I'd give one coffee. Sure, I'm glad she answered the way she did. But I think I could have handled it even if she'd been more angry."

But what about this fear of being thought selfish and indifferent to others? As we've said before, most of us have been brought up to believe that we should consider others' needs first and that, above all, we should not be selfish. Many times women in our groups say, "But if I become assertive, if I say *no* to all the things I don't feel like doing, I'll turn into an egotistical, self-centered woman." We maintain that there is

a difference between choosing to say *yes* to help someone out—even if it means doing something we don't
like to do—and saying *yes* only because we are too
anxious to say *no*. When we *choose* to say *yes* (or *no*)
we are assertive. When we say *yes* by default, because
we don't know how to say *no*, we are non-assertive and
are likely to carry on or project our underlying resentment in some way.

A few weeks after she had completed assertive training we received a letter from Barbara, an energetic,
spirited woman of fifty-five. She had spent most of her
adult life working as a speech therapist and providing
a stable household for a series of foster children. She
wrote of her own struggle to deal assertively with
expressing her own desires:

*I know I'm continuing to grow in my understanding of
the principles of assertive training and the use of those
principles in my life. It's a great feeling to be able to take
care of my own needs too—that was one of the big
hurdles to overcome. My nurturing had included so many
"everyone else first" messages that I felt my strongest beliefs being tested by the idea that I had rights too. I
finally realized that I had believed in taking care of everyone else, but neglecting myself. Now deep inside, I really
believe that I count too. And I have more love left over
for others than I ever thought possible.*

Irrational Belief #6
*At all costs, I must avoid making statements and
asking questions that might make me look ignorant
or stupid.*

Rational Counterpart to #6
*It's all right to lack information or to make a
mistake. It just shows I'm human.*

114

Just as it is irrational to expect everyone to be pleased with us all of the time, it is also irrational to believe that everyone must think we are intelligent all of the time. Some of us are reluctant to express an opinion to or ask a question of people who may appear expert in a given area, even though to fail to do so might deprive us of essential information or cause us unnecessary worry. We operate on the irrational belief that "It would be humiliating if I asked a dumb question. I'd never live it down."

Maria, six months pregnant with her first child, told us how she always took a list of questions to her appointments with the obstetrician. More often than not, she left his office with her questions unanswered. She explained that she knew he was busy, and was afraid that her questions would appear unimportant and ridiculous to him. Meanwhile, her anxiety continued to grow as her questions went unanswered.

Another woman in the group sympathized with Maria and then added, "He's getting paid for his services. You don't need to win his approval. So what if your question is old hat to him—you're not there to show him how smart you are. People don't expect you to know all the answers anyway. So why not find out what you need to know?"

So Maria practiced asking her questions in the assertive training group until she felt ready to present them to the obstetrician. "Just thinking of it that way and practicing makes me feel better. Now it seems foolish *not* to ask my questions."

At her next doctor's visit, Maria found that she could ask questions and get answers. Her success left her feeling good about herself, and she was very relieved to finally have the information she wanted.

Irrational Belief #7

Assertive women are cold, castrating bitches. If I'm assertive I'll be so unpleasant that people won't like me.

Rational Counterpart to #7

Assertive women are direct and honest, and behave appropriately. They show a genuine concern for other people's rights and feelings as well as their own. Their assertiveness enriches their relationships with others.

We may keep ourselves behaving non-assertively through confusing assertiveness with aggressiveness. If we believe the erroneous stereotype that assertive women are cold, unpleasant, castrating women, we are failing to make the distinction between *uncaring domination*, which is *aggression*, and *appropriate communication*, which is *assertion*. We need to bear in mind the image of the assertive woman who is caring and empathic, direct and honest, and who values her own worth.

Helen, a young social worker at a residential treatment center for adolescents, explained how her image of herself was changing and becoming stronger each time she asserted herself. She said, "I used to accept all the feminine stereotypes, and really thought that nobody likes a strong woman. But lately I have come to believe that no one will respect me or my ideas unless I do. I need to stand up for myself."

She then discussed a recent experience from her second week on a new job. "I work with the kids and the teachers at the Center all day, and usually go home around four thirty. Last Wednesday I came back to my office after dinner to catch up on some paperwork. As I got out of my car I bumped right into Ruth, who

116

had held my job for eight years before I took over. I was very surprised to see her there, since I knew she didn't work at the Center any more. So I said, 'Hi, what are you doing here?'

"She told me that there had been a problem in the senior dorm and that the director, Mr. Bemis, had called her to come over and talk to the girls to try to calm things down.

"Well," Helen continued, "I replied to her rather matter-of-factly, but I'll tell you, my heart was racing and I was feeling furious and upset. I didn't know what to make of it. Maybe Mr. Bemis didn't trust me. Perhaps he thought I was too inexperienced . . . or incompetent. And on and on . . .

"I went into my office and thought for a few minutes. I decided that I wanted to tell Mr. Bemis that I was upset and ask him for information. At the same time I was afraid that he might defend his actions by telling me what I feared the most—that he did not consider me competent enough. So I phoned him and told him I wanted to see him as soon as possible—preferably the next morning. He scheduled an appointment for ten A.M.

"When I went to his office I was so nervous my stomach was tied in knots. But I took a deep breath and told him exactly what I had been thinking and feeling. I said something like 'You've been very reassuring during my first two weeks on the job, but I need to tell you about what happened last night.' Then I went on with what had happened.

"While hearing me out Mr. Bemis looked flustered, and his face got red. He said, 'You know, I didn't really take your feelings into account in this, and I have to admit that maybe I've been feeling a little unsure about your competence. We really haven't had much opportunity to work together yet. Then he explained that when the trouble in the dorm arose he had called the Center's psychiatrist, who had referred him to Ruth. Without thinking of me—or the implications—at all, he had asked Ruth to come over.

"He apologized and said he'd try not to let it happen again—and he actually thanked me for being so direct with him. Mr. Bemis was pleased because he knew that I would discuss problems with him before they grew out of proportion. As a result of this discussion, I know our respect for each other increased."

It's not always easy to take risks, real or imagined, in expressing our angry or hurt feelings. Helen had decided that she could talk over what was bothering her without being a "bitch." She knew that she was not intending to dominate or control Mr. Bemis, but essentially to tell him of her distress directly, and to find out the facts. As a result, she felt much better, and the basis for mutual trust was established.

Conclusion

If we want to be assertive, but are stopping ourselves with fear about the outcome of our assertion, then we should examine these possibly irrational aspects of our thinking:

Am I assuming that people will always react negatively to my assertion? *That's irrational.*

Am I focusing on the negative outcome of my assertiveness and not considering other options? *That's irrational.*

Do I think I can't handle the results of my assertive behavior if they are, in fact, negative? *That's irrational.*

Replacing our irrational beliefs with rational ones helps us to reduce our anxiety. It enables us to realistically assess situations in which assertive behavior may or may not be suitable. It gives us the freedom to make intelligent and presumably satisfying—or at least bearable—choices about our own behavior.

Exercise

The following irrational beliefs were discussed in this chapter:

1. If I assert myself, others will become angry with me.
2. If I assert myself and people do become angry with me, I will be devastated; it will be awful.
3. Although I prefer others to be straightforward with me, I'm afraid that if I am open with others and say *no*, I will hurt them.
4. If my assertion hurts others, I am responsible for their feelings.
5. It is wrong and selfish to turn down legitimate requests. Other people will think I'm terrible and won't like me.
6. At all costs, I must avoid making statements and asking questions that might make me look ignorant or stupid.
7. Assertive women are cold, castrating bitches. If I'm assertive I'll be so unpleasant that people won't like me.

Do any of these apply to you? Do you have any others to add?

The following questions may be helpful in enabling you to see your behavior for what it is and try to replace your irrational beliefs with rational ones. First, think of a situation in which you want or need to be assertive, but in which you stop yourself from behaving as you would like. Then consider:

1. Do I stop myself from acting assertively because of beliefs about how I should or shouldn't act in the situation?
2. Are those beliefs true? Do I have any evidence from my own experience to verify them? To contradict them?
3. Do I stop myself from acting assertively because I think that the only outcome would be unpleasant, bad, or wrong? On what evidence?
4. Is that rational, or are there other alternative outcomes? If so, what are they?
5. Do I stop myself from acting assertively for fear that I couldn't possibly handle the results if they should be unpleasant or otherwise problematic?
6. Is that rational? Or can I think of ways that I could actually deal with the possible difficulty?

7

What Is Your Waterloo?— Blocks to Assertiveness

AN important step in learning to act assertively is recognizing those situations which are difficult for us. Some situations will be much more of a problem than others. And, what will be a problem for one woman may not be for another. For instance, you may respond to an angry tirade by becoming meek and compliant, while someone else, who can cope well with angry people, may crumble when someone pleads with her.

In this chapter we will talk about several kinds of situations which typically cause assertiveness problems for women. You might want to keep a journal of those situations which are particularly difficult for you. It may prove valuable later on.

Expressing and Responding to Anger

Expressing our own anger and responding to others' anger toward us is difficult for those of us who have learned that anger is inappropriate, if not taboo. Dealing with anger is often difficult for women, since so many of us have been taught since childhood that it is not ladylike to show our anger.

We may be afraid of what others will think of us if

we express anger. "They won't like me if I get mad!" Or we may fear the power—imagined or real—of our own anger. Consequently, we may deny that we're angry. "No, I'm not mad. I'm just talking loudly to make my point!" We may try to suppress it, hoping that it will subside or disappear. We may mask angry feelings with hurt feelings instead, for many of us have been taught that tears and sadness are more acceptable than anger. Or we may deny our right to be angry. "Thoughtful, mature people don't get angry." "How can I be angry with her? She doesn't really know what she's saying." Such denial ignores the fact that anger is a normal human emotion that we all have.

Consequently, we can accept the appropriateness of our angry feelings and nevertheless decide that if our goal is to *maintain communication and continue an ongoing relationship* with another person, it is possible to express our anger in an assertive way. To be assertive in a situation involving anger *does not mean that we must continually be sympathetic and understanding and smile sweetly*. When we wish to keep the relationship intact it's important to communicate and resolve our anger, rather than to let it build to destructive proportions. *We can let others know directly how we feel and what we want, without attempting to dominate, insult, or humiliate them, without letting the disagreement become a raging battle.*

There are times, of course, when anger is intense and emotions are high, when our primary need is to explode, to alleviate our own tensions, or to end the relationship with the person with whom we are angry. In these circumstances we may want to tell the other person off and forget the consequences. Remember, the purpose of assertive behavior is open, tension-free communication. When we want to unload our anger, when we are not interested in how our anger affects other people, when we want to get back at someone for what he has done, our intent is different; we are not then in a situation calling for assertive behavior.

If we customarily repress our anger in an attempt to keep the peace, our feelings are likely to emerge in indirect ways. Peggy, the soul of punctuality, was upset by others who were habitually late. She hated to wait for Lindsey, an otherwise good friend whose chronic lateness made Peggy more furious each time it happened.

However, instead of telling Lindsey how much she hated to wait for her, Peggy was cool when they finally did meet, and dismissed Lindsey's apologies with a remote "Oh, that's all right." Later she complained to her other friends about Lindsey's lack of courtesy and poor sense of timing. Sometimes she discussed her resentment with the women in her rap group, too, but the fourth time she brought it up one woman got tired of listening to the unproductive commentary and suggested that Peggy talk directly to Lindsey about the problem.

"Oh, I couldn't do that," Peggy said.

"Why not?"

"Lindsey would get mad."

"Well," said the weary listener, "aren't *you* angry about her being late every time it happens?"

Absolutely.

Since her repressed anger and her complaining were self-demeaning and did not resolve the problem, Peggy reluctantly decided that she had to confront Lindsey.

Yet even in expressing her anger Peggy had two options—she could do it *aggressively* or *assertively*.

An aggressive approach would be for Peggy to say,

123

"Lindsey, I've had it! Every time we go somewhere together you're late. You don't even care that I have to wait around for hours. You don't give a damn about anyone but yourself! You're so selfish—I just can't stand it any more!"

Peggy's aggressiveness would put Lindsey on the defensive, with the emphasis on making her feel bad rather than on asking her to change her behavior. "You're always late," "You're inconsiderate," "You're selfish" are the messages. "Waiting around for hours" and "don't give a damn about anyone but yourself" may represent Peggy's impression of Lindsey's behavior, but they are direct attacks on Lindsey and will either put her on the defensive or humiliate her. Peggy would be making it sound as though she'd just as soon end the relationship with Lindsey altogether. Her repeated use of the word "you"—"*You* don't even care," "*You* don't give a damn," "*You're* so selfish"— would label and demean Lindsey.

However, Peggy has another choice: She can express her anger assertively rather than aggressively. She can say, "I like to do things with you, Lindsey, but I feel angry about having to wait for you every time we go somewhere. I'd like you to be ready on time when we go places together. Would you be willing to do that?" This approach *directs the anger to the issue, rather than to the person*. When Peggy says, "I like to do things with you" she specifies the positive side of the friendship first. Then she *states the problem clearly and succinctly*, without unnecessary elaboration or exaggeration. Then she goes on to *make a direct request*, stating what she wants from Lindsey in the future. And she ends with asking Lindsey if she'll go along with this request. Because this assertive approach to the problem assumes the continuity of the friendship and shows that Peggy has a stake in it, it establishes a context for continued, open communication, rather than a prolonged argument and possible disruption of the friendship. Notice that in this assertive expression of anger Peggy *takes responsibility for her own feelings*. Using the pronoun *"I"* instead of *"you,"* Peggy says, "I feel angry," *"I'd* like you to be ready on time." Peggy is expressing her own feelings and desires in tone and manner very different from the accusing, judgmental use of "you" in the previous aggressive statement.

Sometimes just becoming aware that it is possible to express anger assertively rather than aggressively is helpful to women who have difficulty doing this. We need also to recognize the importance of the *timing* of our expression of anger. If we suppress it until we are boiling inside, or if we wait a long time and keep brooding over the issue, it is not going to be easy to be assertive rather than aggressive.

If, on the other hand, we often avoid asserting ourselves for fear of evoking others' anger in retaliation, or of devastating them with our anger, then we will need to figure out whether our fears are rational. We can do this by going through the process described in the preceding chapter on irrational beliefs.

The following questions may help to assess our ways of dealing with anger:

1. Do I usually keep quiet when I'm angry?
2. Do I usually walk away from the other person when I'm angry?
3. Do I simmer for days and then vent my anger in a big blowup?
4. Do I appear to feel hurt when I'm actually angry?

5. Do I take out my anger on someone other than the person at whom I'm angry?
6. Do I express my anger directly and firmly, but without labeling the other person?
7. When someone else is angry with me, can I respond directly and effectively, with composure and without tears? Can I listen, try to understand their grievance?
8. Do I feel hurt and withdraw when someone is angry with me?

Responding to Imperious or Authoritarian Behavior

Some of us find that our main assertiveness problem is in responding suitably to authoritarian behavior in others. We may have learned as children that we should listen to our elders without questioning, that father or teacher or policeman or doctor knows best. For some of us the educational system has reinforced unquestioning acceptance of and respect for authority figures. Because in our society money is often equivalent to power, some of us tend to defer to those who are wealthier than we are. And, as we have seen, women have often been obliged to defer to men. This has been true since the origins of the male-dominated Judeo-Christian and Islamic religions, and carries over today into the laws governing prostitution, birth control, and abortion.

Sure, there are lots of people who know more than we do about some things, but it is unrealistic to confuse authoritativeness with authoritarianism, to assume that all "experts" or people in positions of power or status look down on us, won't give us our say, or will put us down if they have the chance. Some may; they are acting in an authoritarian manner. And often the most powerful people are the least imperious.

Whether the other person's superior attitude is real or imagined by us, if we find ourselves refraining from assertion with people in positions of authority or people who act more authoritative than we feel we are, we are probably selling ourselves short and allowing our rights to be infringed upon. In order to determine whether or not this is happening, it is helpful to examine our behavior with parents, teachers, bosses, and professionals whose services we use. If we find ourselves anxious or reluctant to tell them how we feel, then this is an area where the practice of assertive skills will be useful.

For instance:

1. Can I tell my parents not to visit me?
2. Do I feel free to disagree with my boss?
3. Can I question a grade I or one of my children has received from a teacher?
4. Can I request information that I need from
   a. the Internal Revenue Service?
   b. vocational rehabilitation?
   c. the city or county welfare department?
   d. the bureau of voter registration?
   e. the driver's-license bureau?
   f. an officer of the bank that holds my home mortgage?
5. Can I tell my doctor that I am dissatisfied with some part of his examinations or diagnosis?
6. Can I express my opinion to someone whom I believe to be smarter than I am?
7. Can I confront someone who is in a much more powerful position than I am?
8. Can I make a complaint to the police department?

Refusing Requests

Saying *no* or refusing a request without apologizing and without feeling guilty is extremely difficult for many of us, for it conflicts with much of what we have learned as women in our society. Because many of us expect to be accommodating much of the time, we may find it hard to turn down requests.

For instance, assuming that you *wanted* to be able to refuse the requests in the following situations, could you do so comfortably?

1. A stranger asks to get in front of you in a long ticket line at the movies.
2. An employer expects you to run a personal errand for him during lunch hour or after work.
3. A friend asks you to make a cake for a bake sale.
4. You are invited to chair an important committee in an organization you really value.
5. A male friend pleads with you to go to a play with him. You want to see it, but not with him.
6. Your daughter's Scout executive committee says that without a leader the troop won't be able to meet. Will you do it?
7. A male friend to whom you're strongly attracted pushes you for more sexual intimacy than you want right now.
8. You know that every time Betty drops over unannounced she stays for hours and interrupts your work. You see her coming up your front walk.

If we find ourselves doing many things we don't want to do, participating in a frenzy of activities to which we've become overcommitted, or avoiding people and situations which might lead to requests or demands on our time, we have not yet learned to assert ourselves by saying *no*, and we need practice in this important art.

Making Requests

The same principles that affect our behavior in refusing requests operate in reverse when we make them. If we find it difficult to ask someone else to do something for us, it may be because we don't think we have the right to ask. Or because we fear that others will think they must say *yes*—though in fact they, like ourselves, have the right to refuse. Or because, rationally or not, we expect our requests to be met with a *no*.

Bearing in mind that the person asked has the right to say *yes*—or *no*—to what you ask, would you have trouble in making any of the following requests?

1. Asking a friend to lend you a small amount of money. A large amount. Asking a relative.
2. Asking a friend to run a simple errand for you. A complicated one.
3. Asking a friend to teach you some skill he/she has.
4. Asking your husband to help with the dishes. Cooking. Child care. Household chores. Shopping.
5. Asking someone to listen to a problem you're having.
6. Asking someone you know well to stop behaving in a way that bothers you (such as to stop smoking in your living room).
7. Asking someone you know slightly or not at all to stop the same behavior.

Starting Conversations and
Initiating Communication with Others

Women who have been socially conditioned to be passive, to let others—especially men—take the initiative and make the overtures, may feel hesitant about starting conversations, particularly with strangers or people in authority. In order to understand which situations are most likely to cause anxiety, let's ask ourselves some questions:

1. Do I feel anxious or hesitant about speaking up in groups?
2. If I didn't know anyone at a party, would I start up a conversation with a stranger?
3. Would I call someone I knew only by reputation to get some information?
4. Would I call a neighbor I didn't know well to say that his roving dog was bothering my children?
5. Am I able to give compliments or praise when I think they're deserved? Even to someone I don't know well?

Some of the categories we have discussed in this chapter may present few problems to the reader; others may pose considerable difficulty, as answers to the various preceding questions should reveal.

Answering the following questionnaire should be helpful in a number of ways. It can help you become aware of areas which are *not* problems, and on which you can build. It can also help you recognize your own particular blocks to assertiveness and pinpoint the situations in which it is especially difficult to be assertive. We suggest that you make a note of these in the journal. This in turn will help you to know what you need to practice.

Questionnaire
Blocks to Acting Assertively

The following questionnaire covers six areas that are often blocks to assertive behavior. There are two questions for each area. The first allows you to assess your attitude and irrational beliefs; the second gives you a chance to examine your behavior.

Check one or more answers, as they apply.

Dealing with My Own Anger
1. When I am angry with people I usually:
   a. am afraid to say anything directly, because I don't want to hurt their feelings.
   b. am afraid that if I do say something, it will sound aggressive and they won't like me.
   c. feel O.K. about expressing what is on my mind.
   d. feel anxious and confused about what I want to say.
2. When I am angry with someone I usually:
   a. drop hints about my feelings, hoping he or she will get the message.
   b. tell the person in a direct way what I want, and feel O.K. about it.
   c. avoid the person for a while until I calm down and the anger wears off.
   d. blow up and tell him/her off.
   e. express my anger sarcastically—getting my point across with some humor or a dig.

Dealing with Others' Anger
3. When someone gets angry with me I usually:
   a. think he/she doesn't like me.

b. feel too scared to ask why and to try to work things out.

c. feel confused and want to cry.

d. think I have a right to understand why he/she is angry and to respond to it.

e. immediately feel wronged.

f. feel angry in return.

g. feel guilty.

4. When someone gets angry with me I usually:

a. end up crying.

b. back off.

c. ask him/her to explain his/her anger further, or else I respond to it in some other straightforward manner.

d. get angry in return.

e. apologize if I don't understand why he/she is angry.

f. try to smooth it over.

g. make a joke out of it and try to get him/her to forget the flareup.

Authoritarian Behavior

5. When I need time and information from a busy professional, I usually think he or she will:

a. resent my taking up valuable time.

b. consider my request as legitimate and be pleased that I'm interested.

c. act as though he/she doesn't mind but secretly resent me.

d. make me feel inferior.

6. When I need time and information from a busy professional I usually:

a. put off calling until I absolutely have to.

b. apologize for taking up his/her time when I call.

   c. state directly what I need and ask for what I want.

   d. let him/her know that I expect immediate attention. After all, I'm important too.

Refusing Requests

7. If someone asks me to do a favor for him/her and I refuse, I think he/she probably will:

   a. hate me.

   b. be angry with me.

   c. understand and will not mind.

   d. act as though he/she doesn't mind, but secretly resent me.

   e. think I don't like him/her.

   f. hesitate to ask me again.

8. If someone asks me to do him/her a favor and I don't want to do it, I usually:

   a. do it anyway.

   b. let him/her know that I resent the request, but do it grudgingly.

   c. make up an excuse as to why I can't do it.

   d. tell him/her I'd rather not do it.

   e. tell him/her I'd rather not do it, and apologize profusely.

Making Requests

9. When I need something from someone else, I usually feel:

   a. as though I shouldn't bother him/her by asking.

   b. as though people don't really want to do things for me.

   c. as though I don't want to put him/her on the spot by asking.

   d. that it's O.K. to go ahead and ask.

e. afraid to ask, because he/she might say *no*.

f. as though he/she should do what I want.

10. When I need something from someone else, I usually:

    a. don't ask unless I'm absolutely desperate.

    b. ask and apologetically explain why I need help.

    c. do nice things for him/her, hoping the favor will be returned.

    d. become demanding and insist on getting my way.

    e. ask directly for what I want, knowing that he/she can refuse my request if he/she wants to.

Initiating Communication

11. When I walk into a party where I don't know anyone, I usually think:

    a. that no one there will talk to me.

    b. that everyone else is relaxed except me.

    c. that I'm out of place, and everyone knows it.

    d. that I won't be able to say the right thing if someone does talk to me.

    e. that it will be fun to meet some new people.

    f. of ways to get attention.

12. When I walk into a party where I don't know anyone, I usually:

    a. wait for someone to come and talk with me.

    b. introduce myself to someone who looks interesting.

    c. stay on the sidelines and keep to myself.

    d. put a lampshade on my head or otherwise behave in a bizarre manner, hoping someone will notice.

    e. rush for food or drink or a cigarette to make it look as if I'm busy and having a good time.

The following answers on the questionnaire indicate assertive beliefs and behaviors:

1. c		7. c	
2. b		8. d	
3. d		9. d	
4. c		10. e	
5. b		11. e	
6. c		12. b	

If you didn't do too well, don't worry, nobody's perfect. Look over your answers. On questions where yours were the same as those above, you probably have no trouble in asserting yourself. For those where your answers differ, figure out which of the areas are the most difficult. Then think of specific situations in your life that fit those problem categories. Look at the questionnaire again and try to figure out just what irrational beliefs may be blocking your assertiveness.

8

Away with Anxiety

NON-ASSERTIVE behavior is self-perpetuating. It becomes a part of a cycle that reinforces our low self-esteem. When we are passive even though we want to be assertive, we start feeling bad about ourselves. The worse we feel, the more anxious we become about trying to assert ourselves the next time. This anxiety continues to interfere with our assertive behavior. The cycle looks like this:

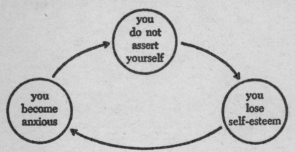

Anxiety inhibits assertive behavior. This is a basic principle of behavioral psychology. Therefore, in order to begin to change and act assertively, we must confront our anxiety and begin to reduce it. But how? The approach on which assertive training is based has us begin by changing our behavior—actually trying out assertive behavior that is likely to bring us positive results. Then, as we begin to get results, our feelings about ourselves begin to change; we become more confident. The more confident we become, the less we tend to be anxious, and the more likely we are to assert ourselves the next time. We can break the old self-defeating cycle by changing our behavior, and as we do, we start a new cycle. It looks like this:

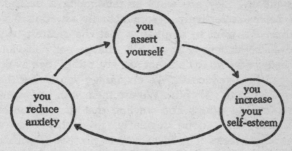

Sybil, an articulate, soft-spoken twenty-six-year-old, had recently been appointed to the executive board of the health-care agency where she worked. She reported that she was self-conscious about being the only woman board member, and that she was unhappy about being so afraid to speak up in the meetings.

"I feel as though everyone is waiting to hear what the token woman will say. I've been so silent that now I actually feel powerless. Decisions are being made that I don't agree with, and I just sit there. The less I speak up, the worse I feel about myself, and the more nervous I feel about saying what I really think. By now the rest of the board probably thinks I'm a dud and wouldn't want to listen to me anyway."

We talked about Sybil's problem in our assertive training group. In the discussion she examined her rights and irrational beliefs, and then decided to play her own role with other members of the group. They acted as the board. The discussion and role playing greatly reduced her anxiety, and she decided to make a real effort to speak out at least twice at the next board meeting. Then we talked about some techniques for anxiety reduction which she could use before going into the meeting.

With practice any one of us can learn these skills. Essentially, they are ways of reinforcing a decision to behave assertively before actually asserting ourselves. We want to emphasize that the greatest way to reduce anxiety is to actually change our behavior. Whatever we do to confront anxiety, rather than avoid it, can help reduce it. We encourage you to try the exercises in this chapter. We use them with our assertive training groups and we find that they are most effective when done regularly, preferably over a period of weeks. The ideal way to practice is with a friend or group of friends who can provide support and reinforcement for your effort.

Exercises in Reducing Anxiety

1. *Imagining a Successful Assertion*

This exercise will help you imagine what it's like to feel successful with your assertion. Giving yourself a positive image of what it would be like to assert yourself can help to reduce your fear of trying it out.

Think of a situation requiring assertiveness, which makes you anxious. Close your eyes. Imagine yourself looking and feeling very self-confident and assertive. Picture yourself carrying out the assertion successfully. Think of one or several rewards you will receive for accomplishing this. Let yourself feel very good about this prospect.

138

2. Covert Messages or Self-Encouragement

Another way to reduce anxiety before beginning an assertion is to devise a message for yourself which will help to get you through the situation. When we ask the women in our groups to do this, most of them are able to come up with potent, encouraging messages. Here are a few examples:

Wendy, who had been putting off refusing an invitation to a party, started telling herself, "If I don't do it now, I'll just have to do it later."

Abby, who wanted her roommate to clean the kitchen, said, "She'll never know what I want unless I tell her."

Other useful messages are:

"I know I have the *right* to do this."

"I don't have to fear the worst will happen."

"I'll feel better about myself if I do it."

a. Now think of a situation that is giving you problems.

b. Think through how you might be stopping yourself from acting assertively. For instance, are you focusing on only the fearful consequences?

c. What kind of strong message can you tell yourself that will enable you to go ahead and act assertively?

d. keep this message and use it from now on. You may want to write it down.

3. Conscious Relaxation

When we are active and exerting ourselves, we breathe from the chest. When we are completely relaxed we usually breathe from the abdomen. If we want to reduce our bodily tension, we can teach ourselves to deliberately breathe from the abdomen and to systematically relax all of our muscles.[8]

It is not sufficient to read about deep breathing techniques, puff out our bellies a few times and breathe deeply while we are reading, and then expect to be able to relax at whim. The only way to understand what this relaxation feels like and to develop confidence in its effectiveness is to try it out repeatedly—to learn to do it.

If we are anticipating a difficult situation, we can practice conscious relaxation before the event; a friend of ours used it before job interviews. Obviously, we can't lie down on the floor and do a conscious relaxation of our entire body on the spot every time we are faced with an anxiety-producing situation calling for assertiveness. However, if we are in the habit of doing conscious relaxation and deep breathing, we can actually relax our bodies considerably by taking several deep abdominal breaths, releasing the tension as we exhale. This is so inconspicuous that no one else need be aware of what we are doing. We can simply pause for a few seconds, take several deep breaths, concentrate on releasing the tension, and stand or sit in a self-confident way, before we begin to speak.

It is important to practice conscious relaxation repeatedly. Through practice our bodies become trained to make the association between abdominal breathing and relaxation, and it is much easier to relax at will with a few breaths.

Have a friend read the following conscious-relaxation exercise aloud to you while you practice it. We suggest that the reader read slowly, except when the instructions say to tighten your muscles.

140

(Afterward you can do the same for her.) Or tape the exercise and play it back for yourself. After you have done it several times, you will probably be able to do it on your own.

Wear loose clothing, and remove your shoes, interfering jewelry, glasses or contact lenses. Find a quiet place with soft lighting where you will be uninterrupted. Lie down on your back—on a rug or a mat or a *firm* bed. Get comfortable.

Now begin. Close your eyes . . . Become aware of your body. Notice any tension in your body . . . Adjust your position to become more comfortable . . . Now become aware of your breathing . . . Inhale slowly through your nose . . . Exhale even more slowly through your mouth . . . Inhale . . . Exhale . . . Find your own pace . . . Let your breathing regulate itself . . . Let yourself pause as long as is comfortable between breaths . . . Exhale . . .

Become aware of all the thoughts going through your head right now . . . Picture a blackboard, and imagine that all your thoughts are written on a blackboard . . . See yourself taking an imaginary eraser and slowly erasing the blackboard . . .

Now, focus on your body. Place your hand on your abdomen . . . Breathe deeply from the abdomen . . . Your abdomen should inflate like a balloon as you inhale and deflate as you exhale.

Inhale slowly through your nose, inflating your abdomen . . . Exhale more slowly through your mouth, letting your abdomen relax . . . Inhale . . . Exhale . . . Inhale . . . Exhale . . . As you exhale think of releasing all the tension from your body . . . Inhale . . . Exhale . . . Let all the tension disappear.

Now continue your rhythmic breathing. Remove your hand from your abdomen and place it on the floor [or bed]. Make sure you are comfortable. Keep this position throughout the rest of the exercise.

Now tense your entire body slightly except for your neck and face. Hold your breath and clench your fists. Contract your muscles. Feel the tension in your shoulders, your arms, your hands, your chest . . . back . . . abdomen . . . pelvis . . . buttocks . . . thighs . . . calves . . . feet . . . and toes. Tense all your muscles . . . Your back is arched. Your limbs are tensed. Now, exhale—let go of all the tension and R E L A X.

Breathe deeply from the abdomen . . . Then slowly exhale . . . Breathe deeply again and . . . exhale.

Now, breathe in. Hold your breath and tense your muscles again. This time, tense them harder with a medium level of tension. Clench your fists. Contract all your muscles. Feel the tension in your shoulders, your arms, your hands, your chest, back, abdomen, pelvis, buttocks, thighs, feet, and toes. All your muscles feel tense. Your body is tight. Hold it! Now, exhale and relax all your muscles. Let go and let the tension flow out.

Breathe deeply from the abdomen . . . and . . . exhale . . . Inhale . . . Exhale . . . Let all the tension leave your body . . . Inhale . . . Exhale . . .

Now . . . inhale . . . Hold your breath and contract your muscles as tightly as you can. Clench your fists. Feel the tension in your shoulders, your arms, hands, chest, back (your back is arched off the floor). Feel the tension in your abdomen, pelvis, buttocks, thighs, calves, feet, and toes. Tense all your muscles as tightly as you can. Your body is trembling with the tension . . . Now, exhale . . . Release your muscles and R E L A X . . .

Inhale from the abdomen . . . and . . . exhale . . . Inhale . . . Exhale . . .

All the tension is leaving your body. Inhale . . . Exhale . . . Inhale . . . Exhale . . . Feel the tension flowing from your body each time you breathe . . . Inhale . . . Exhale . . . Inhale . . . Exhale . . . Let all distracting thoughts leave your mind. Just concentrate on your body. Continue your abdominal breathing . . .

Now focus your attention on your head. Be aware of the top of your head . . . feel all the tension flowing out your head and forehead . . . relax the upper part of your head . . . let your head become completely relaxed. [Pause.]

Become aware of your jaw . . . let it go slack . . . all the tension is leaving your jaw . . . your whole head . . . Your eyes . . . your face . . . are relaxed . . . Be aware of the relaxed feeling . . . your head is without tension . . . totally free . . . [Pause.]

Now concentrate on your neck . . . Focus on it and let it relax . . . Continue to breathe deeply . . . continue to relax . . .

Now focus your attention on your shoulders . . . Feel your shoulders relax . . . They don't have to support anything . . . let all the tension flow out of them . . . let your shoulders relax completely . . . Continue to inhale . . . and exhale . . .

Concentrate now on your arms . . . Be aware of their position and of all the tension flowing out of them . . . let your arms relax. All the tension is flowing down your arms through your hands and your fingers . . . right out through your finger tips. Feel your arms, your hands, and your fingers become totally relaxed . . . Continue to breathe deeply . . . Inhale . . . Exhale . . . Inhale . . . Exhale . . .

Now become aware of your back. The floor [or bed] is providing total support for your back . . . your back can relax completely . . . Let all the tension flow out of your back . . .

Now focus your attention on your chest . . . let your chest and your rib cage relax totally . . . Be aware of the relaxed feeling in your chest . . . it is totally without tension . . .

Be aware of your back being relaxed and free . . . Continue to breathe in and exhale . . . The whole upper part of your body is totally without tension . . . Enjoy being aware of the relaxation of your upper body . . . It is completely free of tension . . . it is relaxed . . .

Concentrate, now, on your lower back and your buttocks. Let them relax . . . All the tension is flowing out . . . Relax your lower back right to the tip of your spinal column. Relax your buttocks . . . Continue to breathe deeply. Inhale . . . Exhale . . .

Become aware of your pelvis and your genitals. Focus your attention on your pelvis. Let your pelvis relax . . . All the tension is leaving . . .

Now focus on your thighs . . . feel them relaxing . . . all the tension is leaving your thighs. . .

Now, your knees and calves. Your knees feel suspended . . . they are without pressure . . . relax your calves . . . let them be totally at rest . . . the tension is flowing out of your knees and your calves . . . your legs are totally relaxed.

Focus on your ankles . . . your ankles are without strain . . . let them totally relax . . . Continue to breathe deeply . . . All the tension is gone from your legs and your ankles . . .

Now become aware of your feet . . . Much of the day your feet bear the weight of your body . . . Now they are without pressure . . . be aware of your arches . . . of the balls of your feet . . . your feet are relaxed . . . let them float free . . . Be aware of your toes . . . the last bit of tension in your body is flowing out through your toes . . . Let your toes completely relax . . . Continue to breathe evenly . . . slowly . . . and deeply . . .

Your whole body is completely relaxed . . . Be aware of the feeling of peace and relaxation . . . total relaxation. Enjoy the sensation of total relaxation . . . total concentration on yourself.

Continue to breathe deeply . . . let yourself float . . .
[Long pause.]
When you feel like it, stretch, and slowly sit up.

144

When you've finished you're likely to feel a tingling sensation over your entire body. If you were able to relax totally you are probably aware of how different complete relaxation feels from our usual state of mild physical tension. If it was difficult to consciously relax each body part, we urge you to repeat it until it gets easier. Each time you do it, you will find it easier to relax. Practice often and regularly.

9

Body Language
Says More than You Think

EXPERTS estimate that 65 percent of our communication is non-verbal and only 35 percent of it is verbal. Much of our non-verbal communication is unconscious, some of it is unintentional, yet most of it is understood. "Non-verbal communication," sometimes called "body language," is a term that broadly encompasses not only gestures, facial expressions, posture, and body movements, but tone and pitch of voice, rate of speaking, habitual mannerisms, appropriate or inappropriate laughter, and lots more.

We learn at an early age to express our pleasure by smiling and our displeasure by pouting or crying. As adults we may continue consciously to express ourselves in these ways. At other times we are unaware of what our non-verbal behavior is communicating, for it's hard to see and hear ourselves from another's vantage point. So part of the intention of this chapter is to help us to become aware of those aspects of our non-verbal communication that affect our assertiveness.

It is ten P.M., and Brenda, a weary architecture student, is about to settle down on her couch to read a book and relax. She is exhausted and is looking forward to enjoying some peace at last. She stretches out on the soft pillows of her sofa, pulls an afghan over her legs, and is just about to take a sip of chilled wine when she hears a blast of rock music from the apartment overhead. She winces at the loud sounds, mutters to herself, and sinks back into the sofa—trying to ignore the intruding distraction. After a few minutes it becomes obvious to Brenda that she cannot escape the noise. She decides that the music is unlikely to be turned down unless she asks her upstairs neighbors to do so. She reluctantly pulls herself up out of her warm, comfortable spot, puts on her shoes, trudges upstairs, and rings the buzzer.

Ellen and Jerry answer the door. The music is on full blast, and they are overheated, smiling; they obviously have been dancing and enjoying it. Brenda says "Hello," and then: "You may not realize it, but the music is coming through into my apartment. It's really bothering me, and I'd like you to turn it down."

When we read what Brenda said, it looks like a very effective assertive statement. She has included empathy and a statement of how she feels and what she wants.

But we cannot accurately classify Brenda's behavior merely by looking at the words. The non-verbal aspects of communication—such as the ways people speak, gesture, and move—play a large part in how the message is transmitted. Even if a verbal statement seems direct and appropriate, its impact is diminished or exaggerated if the non-verbals are not congruent.

Let's look at the non-verbal messages in Brenda's statement.

147

Non-Assertive Non-Verbal Communication

When Ellen and Jerry open the door, they find Brenda standing there with her shoulders stooped, her head down, shifting from one foot to the other. She doesn't look at either of them, and when she begins to speak her voice sounds soft and hesitant, with long pauses in between the words. She clasps her hands in front of her, and looks tense and apologetic. She says:

"You . . . uh . . . may not . . . realize it,	*Said very softly and hesitantly*
but the music is . . . uh . . . coming through into my apartment.	*Said very softly, with the pace increasing as she proceeds, as if to get it over with*
It's really bothering me,	
and I'd like you to turn it down?"	*Ends request with a question, followed by nervous laughter.*

Here Brenda is stating how she feels and what she wants, but her hesitant voice, averted eyes, questioning inflection, nervous gestures, and laughter convey a double message, which essentially says, "I want you to turn the music down, but it's not that important. I'm not sure I have the right to ask you. Don't take me too seriously."

Aggressive Non-Verbal Communication

If Brenda spends two hours lying on her couch, unsuccessfully trying to read and relax, before she finally decides to ask the neighbors to turn down their music, it is very possible that she will react aggressively. By being non-assertive for a considerable time, by sitting and hoping that the music will stop, by denying her own desires and needs, Brenda probably will build up hostility. It may go as follows:

Brenda slams her book down on the table and storms up the stairs. She knocks loudly on Ellen and Jerry's door. When they open it they see her standing with her hands on her hips, and her face set in a cold and angry stare. She begins to speak in a tense, loud, demanding voice, emphasizing certain words that accent its accusing severity:

"*You* may not realize it,	*Sneering.*
but the music *is* coming through into *my* apartment. It's really *bothering* me,	*Spoken quickly, with increasing emphasis, except when the pace of the last words slows for dramatic effect.*
and *I'd like you to turn it down!*"	

Obviously, the same words said in this manner have an entirely different effect from the earlier non-assertive delivery. When Brenda communicates in an aggressive manner, she intends to convey not only a request to turn down the music, but anger and hostility. She wants to tell Jerry and Ellen off and make them feel guilty. The words are still "correctly assertive," but the non-verbal message is the more powerful, and it is clearly aggressive.

Assertive Non-Verbal Communication

Let's take Brenda back to her apartment and give her one more chance. This time she settles onto the couch,

149

pulls up the afghan, and is about to take a sip of chilled wine. The music suddenly blasts forth, and she thinks to herself, "Wow, I'll never get any rest this way. I'd better ask them to turn it down."

She puts on her shoes and walks up the stairs. As she faces the door she stands up straight and knocks firmly, a few times. When they open the door, Ellen and Jerry see Brenda standing there, facing them directly, her hands relaxed at her sides.

She looks at them and in a firm, warm well-modulated voice says,

"You *may* not realize it,
but the *music* is coming through into my apartment.
It's *really* bothering me,
and I'd like you to turn it down."

Brenda is relaxed, but she does not laugh or disqualify her message in any way. She makes the request in a way that indicates that she expects to be taken seriously. Her body and voice, as well as her words, make that communication convincing.

It is often more difficult to learn the non-verbal components of assertive behavior than the verbal ones, perhaps because it is relatively easy to remember the words we're prepared to say, but harder to refrain from unconscious mannerisms.

In our assertive training groups, we ask women to give each other feedback not only on what they say but also on how they say it. On our own, *we can get feedback by asking for it from others, watching ourself in the mirror, using a tape recorder,* or deciding consciously to *assess what our body is doing when we try out assertive behavior.*

In the first few sessions, members of our groups

often tell us that they have tried out assertive behavior but their attempt has been relatively ineffective.

In demonstrating such a situation to the group, Gloria's words were beautifully assertive, but her non-verbal accompaniments were silently but clearly saying "Don't pay attention to me." Members of the group pointed out her timid and hesitant voice, nervous gestures, and evasive looks, and asked her to *stand up straight*, to *speak in a well-modulated voice*, and to *look directly at the person she was addressing*. They told her to *think about her rights* and to *speak as though she expected others to take her seriously*. Even with these directions Gloria still spoke meekly, avoided eye contact, and came across non-assertively.

Finally we asked her to say what she wanted assertively, but to do it in a way that she considered exaggerated. After we told her to exaggerate all her gestures, she stood up straight, looked her partner in the eye, and directly and firmly made her statement. When she finished, we asked her how she felt about what she had just done. She said, "Oh, that was so extreme. I'm sure people wouldn't like me if I actually did that."

Before she could even finish speaking, practically the entire group of women, leaders included, took issue with her interpretation, for all had seen her behavior not as overdone but as appropriately assertive. The group pointed out that she hadn't been abrupt or domineering, but direct and straightforward—in posture, gestures, and tone of voice, as well as in words.

Gloria, like so many of us, had learned over the years to be as non-threatening and agreeable as possible. Whether making requests or defending her rights, she spoke softly and hesitantly, or laughed off her own statements. Only through exaggerating her behavior in her mind was Gloria actually able to be assertive, and to train herself to develop new patterns of behavior. Over time, with repeated practice—in front of a mirror, with group members, and with friends—Gloria began to be comfortable in behaving assertively in non-verbal as well as verbal ways.

Exaggeration can be a useful technique to help us to push ourselves into being assertive, as long as we also learn to feel and recognize the differences in our uses of body and voice when we are being assertive and when we are not. Getting feedback on our behavior from friends is important in helping to establish a balance that is both comfortable and assertive.

The following chart, adopted from the work of Dr. Margaret Fagin of the University of Missouri–St. Louis, summarizes the verbal and non-verbal components of non-assertive, assertive, and aggressive behavior, and is a useful reference in recognizing and distinguishing among these.

We can see that non-assertive behavior is filled with many cues which imply, "I'm not important. Ignore me." They may reinforce self-effacing words. Or there may be discrepancies between the words and the non-verbal accompaniment. For example, if someone says, in a weak, halting voice, "I don't mind loaning you ten dollars," and scuffs the ground, then looks down at it as she speaks, the message is confusing. The listener has to choose between the verbal and the non-verbal messages. If the listener merely takes the ten dollars and says, "Thanks," the speaker may be left feeling resentful. "Couldn't she tell I didn't really want to loan it to her?"

Verbal and Non-Verbal Components of Behaviors

	NON-ASSERTIVE	ASSERTIVE	AGGRESSIVE
I. VERBAL	Apologetic words. Veiled meanings. Hedging; failure to come to point. Rambling; disconnected. At loss for words. Failure to say what you really mean. "I mean," "you know."	Statement of wants. Honest statement of feelings. Objective words. Direct statements, which say what you mean. "I"-messages.	"Loaded" words. Accusations. Descriptive, subjective terms. Imperious, superior words. "You"-messages, that blame or label.
II. NON-VERBAL **A. General**	Actions instead of words, hoping someone will guess what you want. Looking as if you don't mean what you say.	Attentive listening behavior. General assured manner, communicating caring and strength.	Exaggerated show of strength. Flippant, sarcastic style. Air of superiority.
B. Specific **1. Voice**	Weak, hesitant, soft, sometimes wavering.	Firm, warm, well-modulated, relaxed	Tense, shrill, loud, shaky, cold, "deadly quiet"; demanding, superior, authoritarian.
2. Eyes	Averted; downcast, teary, pleading.	Open, frank, direct. Eye contact, but not staring.	Expressionless; narrowed; cold; staring; not really "seeing" you.
3. Stance and posture	Lean for support; stooped; excessive head nodding.	Well-balanced, straight-on; erect, relaxed	Hands on hips; feet apart. Stiff & rigid, rude, imperious.
4. Hands	Fidgety, fluttery, clammy.	Relaxed motions.	Clenched; abrupt gestures; finger-pointing; fist pounding.

In aggressive behavior the verbal and non-verbal elements may or may not reinforce each other. Whether or not the words are hostile or neutral, the gestures are domineering and intrusive. Non-verbal aggressive behavior can be remote, cold, rude, controlled, and superior.

In assertive behavior, on the other hand, the verbal and non-verbal behavior are congruent and reinforce each other. Both are direct, open, and free of anxiety; both communicate the speaker's real message, and should therefore be quite clear.

Exercises

Because many of our non-verbal behaviors and our responses to the non-verbal behavior of others are unconscious, it is helpful to be aware of what we are doing or reacting to. The following exercises can help build your awareness. They will be much more effective if you actually practice them than if you just read about them. They can be done alone, with taped directions, or, with a friend who will read the directions to you.

EXERCISE I

Purpose: To experience the physical feelings (and their psychological components) of a non-assertive stance, an aggressive stance, and an assertive stance.

A. Think of a situation in which you have trouble asserting yourself. Close your eyes for a few seconds and picture yourself being non-assertive; then open your eyes.

Now, get up and walk around the room. Let your shoulders droop. Look down at the ground.

154

Now, stop. Feel the tension in your stomach. You may want to lean on something. Your feet are restless. You have the weight of the world on your shoulders. Feel the burden. You have no rights! Who would listen to you? Let yourself feel the anxiety, the pressure, the frustration of not being able to ask for what you want.

Now, stop! Think for a few seconds about what that felt like. Then, clear your mind.

B. Now, move into an aggressive stance. Think of a situation in which you would feel aggressive, perhaps something about which you've been holding back your anger for a long time. Now, stand up. Clench your fists. Tighten your stomach. Narrow your eyes until they feel hard and cold. Stamp your feet, or plant them firmly on the floor. With your hands on your hips, march or stomp around thinking, "I'll get even with them. They'll be sorry. They'd better look out!"

Now, stop and think for a few seconds about how that felt. Then, clear your mind.

C. Now assume an assertive stance. Stand up straight, shoulders back, head up. Look directly ahead. You are erect but also comfortable, relaxed, attentive, and balanced. Stand there and think to yourself, "I'm about to enter a situation feeling good about myself, knowing what my rights are, and believing I have the right to do what I intend to do. I'll be able to handle it suitably. I feel comfortable and strong about this."

Now, stop and think for a few seconds about how that felt. Then, clear your mind.

D. Now answer the following questions for yourself or discuss them with your partner:

How did you feel in each of these roles? Which

was the easiest role to get into? Did you become aware of body clues that were familiar? How can you use these clues more to help you recognize what you're feeling and how you're acting in specific situations?

Think of ways in which you could move from the physical stance of non-assertion or aggression to the physical stance of assertion.

Take an assertive stance again, and review for yourself what it feels like.

EXERCISE II

Say each of the following statements in three ways: assertively, non-assertively, and aggressively. Be aware of the ways the non-verbal behaviors change the message. If you are doing this exercise with a friend, see if she can guess which kind of behavior you are attempting to demonstrate as you act.

a. I'm returning your book.
b. Sure, you can borrow my sweater.
c. I don't mind.
d. I'd rather do it my way.
e. I don't want to do it for you.
f. Isn't she nice!

10

Learning to Listen

LISTENING well is an important part of open, two-way communication. It reduces the anxiety that keeps us from asserting ourselves, because if we really listen to what the other person is saying, we will be paying attention to them instead of worrying about or silently rehearsing our reply. Also, when the other person feels that he is being listened to he is much more likely to listen to us. In this sense, good listening skills can pave the way for assertive behavior to be well received.

This chapter will also discuss empathic replies, or ways of reflecting back what the other person has said to let him or her know we've heard correctly and understood. This reduces anxiety particularly in a situation where we've been saving up resentments and are now afraid to be assertive for fear that we may lash out and later regret it. And too, good listening reduces the likelihood of misunderstandings.

Jan, a college student living at home, told our assertive training group, "When I got home from our first assertive training class, I walked in the door and my father immediately started giving me his usual speech about how he expected my grades to improve this semester. So I decided to assert myself. I told

157

him that I didn't want him to criticize my grades any more. I was honest and straightforward—just like you said. And I didn't beat around the bush—I just came right out and told him that I didn't like it, and I wanted him to stop.

"But do you know what *he* did? Dad put down my grade reports, straightened up, and said, 'Why shouldn't I worry about your grades? I'm paying for your future by sending you to college, aren't I? If you don't like it, you can stop going to school and get a job!'

"I snapped back," Jan said, "and that was the beginning of another long argument on the same old subject. How did I get into that again, when I was so sure that this time I could prevent a big blowup?"

Several other group members said they knew just what Jan meant. Some had simply stated what they wanted, directly, and had gotten good results. But others found that when they tried to do the same, it didn't work. What happened? What could Jan have done instead?

We asked Jan to demonstrate in class exactly what had gone on so we could examine the total communication more closely.

First Demonstration

FATHER [played by group leader]: Jan, before a new semester starts, I just want you to know that I expect you to get better grades than you have in the past. Your mother and I know what a bright girl you are and—

JAN [played by herself] [interrupting]: Look, Dad, you're never satisfied. I'm old enough to take

158

care of myself. My grades are my business. I want you to *stop* nagging me.

CYNTHIA [another member of the group]: Your father may be coming on a little strong, but it sounds as though he really cares about you and how you do in school. But wow, you came on so abruptly that you were squared away for a battle right from the start.

JAN: Yeah. I know that. Dad really does care. But God, I hate it when he nags me about grades.

CYNTHIA: Well, you could let him know that you realize he's concerned, that you understand what he wants. Then you could tell him how you feel— but without a verbal attack!

Second Demonstration

JAN: O.K. Let me try again. I guess I could say [playing herself], Dad, I know you really care about me; that you want me to get good grades. It sounds as if you're afraid I'll pull a two-point again, and you're angry.

FATHER: Yes, I *am* afraid you'll do that. But I'm not angry—just upset that you're not working up to capacity and that this will affect your chances of getting a good job later on.

JAN: O.K. I know you're just thinking about me. But every time you nag me I feel like a two-year-old. I'm responsible for my own work—and I'd like you to stop pressuring me.

FATHER: O.K. We'll try it your way—for a while. But about those grades . . .

JAN [firmly and directly]: But, Dad, you just said . . .

FATHER: O.K., I'll stop.

The group agreed that this was much more effective, and we began to examine the reasons why. Assertiveness in personal relationships usually involves the *active* communication of our ideas, feelings, and wants. However, there is often more to the assertion than merely saying what you want.

The main problem in Jan's case was that her abrupt interruption, as well as her words, had not set the atmosphere for open communication. Jan was ignoring her father's concern and wasn't really hearing what he was saying. She interrupted him when she became defensive.

If she had practiced skillful assertive communication, as a responsive listener as well as a sender of messages, Jan could have helped to create the climate for a reciprocal discussion, as the Second Demonstration indicates, instead of an argument. Let's take a look at the specific listening skills which Jan—or any of us—could use to improve communication.

Attentive Listening

Attentive listening is simply conveying non-verbally that you are *paying careful attention to someone who is speaking*. It usually involves positioning yourself to make it easier to concentrate on the other person. This includes *looking at the speaker, sitting or standing in a relaxed, attentive position*, and *avoiding distractions*. All of us have probably had the disconcerting experience of being in a crowded room talking with someone who appeared to be constantly looking around—almost anywhere except at us—to see what he was missing, a visual put-down certainly not conducive to good communication.

Short Encouraging Responses

These are very short utterances, such as "Tell me more," "Ummmm-hmmmm," "And then?", or the repetition of one or two key words that the speaker has just used. Their purpose is to encourage the speaker to continue to talk and feel heard. Just a few words can let the speaker know you're with her, without interrupting the flow of talk or breaking the mood. When we really are listening, we can use these short responses without thinking about them.

Reflection of Content and Underlying Feelings

It is often important to indicate not only that we're listening to the speaker, but that we *understand* what she's really saying. One very effective way to do this is to *paraphrase the essence of what the speaker has said*, and to *reflect* it back to her. This is called *reflection of content*. The listener can also reflect back the underlying feelings that come across by responding to words and non-verbal behavior that reveal feelings. This is called *reflection of feelings*. When the emotions or feelings are stronger than what the words actually convey, it's usually better to reflect the feeling to let the person know that you've understood what she's meant. The basic reasons for reflecting are to let the other person know you're really listening, and to *check out* the meaning of what she's said.

It is helpful to keep our reflections tentative as a way of checking to make sure we've heard and understood correctly. This also keeps us from becoming judgmental or analytical. A way of staying tentative

161

as we check and reflect is to begin with one of the following phrases: "Sounds as if you're feeling/thinking/saying . . .", "It seems that you feel . . ." (using a tentative voice inflection); "I'm wondering if you feel . . ."; "Is what you're saying . . ." These phrases may sound stilted as we begin to use them. Nevertheless, as we grow accustomed to paraphrasing and responding empathically, we will be less self-conscious about such phrases, and will ultimately develop our own style of integrating reflections into our responses.

Thus, when Jan said, "It sounds as if you're afraid I'll pull a two-point again, and you're angry," what she thought she heard was not entirely what her father meant to convey; he wasn't angry, but he was upset. However, the reflection was perfectly appropriate, even though Jan was partly wrong. It gave her father a chance to correct the misinterpretation and also the opportunity to clarify by telling her what he really meant. And when Jan told her father, "I know you're just thinking about me," not only did she let him know that she was paying attention and understood his message, she also implied, "What you say matters enough for me to give you my attention and to make sure that I am hearing you accurately."

Obviously, not all conversations require reflective listening skills. If someone asks for information— "Can you direct me to Memorial Drive?"—it would be laughable to reply, "Sounds like you're looking for Memorial Drive." Much of our daily conversation which conveys information, explanations, anecdotes, tales, jokes, and witty repartee involves exchanges that do not necessarily require attentive listening and empathic responses. In many situations these skills may or may not be useful. In social gatherings, for instance, where the conversation is fun and funny, it would be ludicrous if we suddenly started soberly and earnestly to practice reflective listening.

These skills are most useful and suitable in personal discussions involving deep issues, in solving conflicts, and in clarifying communication. They are valuable in any friendship or helping relationship, in dealing with children and other members of our families, and in teaching or leading discussions. *They are valuable when we want to make an assertion that involves understanding the other person's rights as well as our own.*

Exercise in Reflection

Assume in each instance that the opening statement is made by someone talking directly to you. After each statement, you have three possible answers. Select one or more which you think reflect the content or feeling level most accurately, or are the most suitable. Cover each group of responses before you reply to a given statement, and remove the cover to check your answer.

1. *"If the phone rings one more time this morning, I'll scream."*
   a. "Don't get upset about it. Just be glad you're so busy and popular."
   b. "You poor thing. You're so patient to put up with so many distractions. I don't know how you can stand it."
   c. "You've had it with that phone ringing."

Answers:
   a. Advice on how to feel, furthered by reassurances that what's causing the speaker to want to

scream is normal, so she should stop being bothered.

b. Sympathy and praise.

c. Reflection of feeling.

2. *"Mom, you're too busy working all the time. We never have any fun around here."*

a. "What do you mean, 'we don't have fun'? We went to the movies last night and we're going ice skating tomorrow."

b. "You sound a little mad with how things have been going around here."

c. "Why don't you invite Jody to come over and play? That would be fun."

Answers:

a. This defensive statement will probably evoke an argumentative answer.

b. Reflection of feeling. This can create a climate for the speaker to express her feelings in an empathic atmosphere, and can then lead to looking for ways to solve the problem.

c. A suggestion or bit of advice that tries to solve a problem without hearing the feelings involved, and therefore without understanding what the problem is.

3. *"It's two weeks to pay day, and I'm down to five dollars. Why does this always happen to me every month?"*

a. "Constantly working to make ends meet seems to be getting to you."

b. "Why don't you borrow some money from Jane? She just got a raise."

c. "This happens because you don't budget. You should try to stretch your salary out over the whole month."

164

Answers:

    a. Reflection of feeling.

    b. Advice from a problem-solver.

    c. This reply misses the remark; in taking the question literally, it provides information (which the speaker probably knows, anyway) and ignores the feeling expressed in the question.

4. *"Where's Ms. Hyatt's office?"*

    a. "I don't know."

    b. "You're looking for Ms. Hyatt?"

    c. "You seem confused about where to go."

    d. "Up the stairs, turn right, and it's the third door on the left."

Answers:

    a. An honest, straightforward answer.

    b. Reflection of content; not appropriate or helpful here.

    c. Inappropriate reflection of feeling. This was a direct request for information.

    d. Providing information in response to a direct request for it.

5. *"I made some good suggestions at the meeting, and no one picked up on any of them."*

    a. "You sound really hurt about it."

    b. "I know just how you feel. Those men never pay attention to a woman's ideas."

    c. "Why didn't you tell them that you were upset with them?"

Answers:

    a. This is checking your interpretation of the feeling. Even if you are not accurate (for the speaker could reply, "No, I'm not hurt, I'm angry!") it is still appropriate to raise the point and let the other person clarify.

b. This is commiserating, sympathizing, and encouraging the unhappiness, instead of being empathic in a way that will help the speaker solve her own problem.

c. This sounds like a good suggestion. In fact, it may be. But it is also advising and not allowing the speaker to continue to express her feelings. In answering you, she might explain why she couldn't have taken your advice. Or she might agree that she should have done what you suggested and feel unhappy for not having done so at the meeting.

6. *"I have so much work to do for school that I'll never get through the week."*

   a. "Uh, I know just what you mean. I've got three exams and two papers due, my typewriter's broken, and I still have to work twenty hours this week waiting tables."
   b. "You seem harried from all that pressure."
   c. "You don't need to worry. I know you'll get it done—you always come through."

Answers:

   a. One-upping. In this way you let the speaker know that you identify with the problem, but you also remove the focus from her and put it on yourself—where it doesn't belong.
   b. Empathizing with the feelings.
   c. Reassuring and advising, and also discounting what the speaker is really expressing—her feelings.

11

Putting It All Together—
Building Assertive Skills

"**I** KNOW *you're in the mood to go out tonight but I'm very tired and I'd just like to stay home.*"—*wife to her husband*

"*I realize that you're anxious to have all these letters go out today, but I can't possibly do all of them plus all the work you asked me to do on the Johnson report. Can you let me know what your priorities are?*"—*secretary to her boss*

"*I bought this radio here last week, but it isn't working properly and I'd like to exchange it. Here's the sales slip.*"—*customer to salesperson*

Now we should be ready to turn to the actual practice of assertive skills. In getting ready to assert yourself here are some things to keep in mind:

a. Let the other person know you hear and understand him.
b. Let the other person know how you feel.
c. Tell him/her what you want.

Not all of our assertions call for *a* and *b*. Some are simple declarative statements or requests. But in more complicated situations it is a good idea to keep all three of these in mind.

Role playing is at the very heart of the change process in our assertive training groups. Role playing helps us to think through our goals and sharpen specific skills, such as listening, direct expression of feelings and wants, and eye contact. It helps to reduce our anxiety about being assertive, and it helps give us the confidence and courage to try our assertiveness in real-life situations.

Remember, becoming assertive is a building process. It is important to start with situations that don't involve a lot of risk and work up to more difficult ones. This way, chances are better of having positive experiences that will help build your confidence and reduce your anxiety.

The particular kind of role playing we use is called behavior rehearsal,[9] and it is made up of a three-step process:

1. You play yourself and the leader plays the other person.
2. You play the other person, the leader plays you.
3. You play yourself again, and the leader plays the other person.

First we ask the group member to describe the situation she wants to work on. We help her to clarify her goals, and to think of ways to overcome her blocks to assertion. Then we start the role playing. As we said, first the group member plays herself and the leader plays the other person. Then they switch.

When playing the role of the group member, the leader acts assertively, and the group member is free to give the leader as difficult a time as she wants to. This way she can act out her worst fears of how the other person might respond to her.

Finally they switch roles again, giving the group

member a chance to be assertive a second time. This time she can use what she has learned in the second role play. If this rehearsal still doesn't seem to be effective, the two can go on switching roles back and forth, until the group member has found a way of dealing with the situation that she considers satisfactory.

In between each role play the rest of the group analyzes what they have seen, and they discuss the non-verbal and verbal aspects of the assertive response. Each time a woman rehearses her assertive behavior, it gets easier and smoother and she becomes more comfortable and less anxious. After she is satisfied with her role playing we encourage her to promise to try out this new behavior during the coming week. Let's see how it works.

Jane wants to borrow Sandra's sleeping bag for a camping trip. Sandra doesn't want to lend it; in the past she had often allowed friends to borrow her camping equipment, but she began to realize that it was getting worn out from so much use, and that she was starting to resent the borrowers. So, although she has no particular reason to believe that Jane will be irresponsible, Sandra has decided not to lend her equipment any more.

So, when Sandra told the group that Jane had left a telephone message that she wanted to borrow her sleeping bag, we were eager to hear what she was going to do. Sandra agreed to rehearse her behavior with a group leader, and here is what happened.

Role Play I

First the leader asked Sandra to describe Jane so she could learn enough about Jane's behavior to be able to play her part. Sandra was asked to play herself.

SANDRA [as herself, telephoning Jane]: Hi, Jane. How are you?

JANE [played by leader]: Fine. I'm so excited about the camping trip this weekend that I can hardly wait to go. Did you get my message about the sleeping bag?

SANDRA [voice drops]: Well . . . yes, I did . . . You know, Jane, I'd love to loan you the sleeping bag . . . [Sandra really would not love to at all.] but, well . . . I'm trying to stop loaning out so many things . . . You know, I get worried about what might happen to my equipment . . . I know it sounds silly [apologetic], but . . . uh . . . I guess I have a hang-up about it or something . . . I'd really rather not.

JANE: Oh, Sandra, I understand you're worried, but I'll be extra careful.

SANDRA: Jane, I feel terrible saying . . . I don't want you to think I'm selfish, but I guess I'd rather not. I'm really sorry.

JANE: Well, if that's the way you feel about it, Sandra. I'm sure I can borrow one from somebody else.

SANDRA: I hope you understand . . . I'm really sorry . . .

At this point we stopped the dialogue. The group praised Sandra for her attempt to be assertive, for she had in fact said *no*. But Sandra said that she wasn't satisfied. She felt as though she had been unnecessarily apologetic—and scared. The group members agreed.

Role Play II

Then Sandra and the leader switched roles. This time Sandra played her friend Jane and the leader played Sandra.

SANDRA [played by leader]: Hi, Jane. How are you?

JANE [played by Sandra]: Just fine. Hey, did you get my message about the sleeping bag? I can't wait to go on that camping trip this weekend, and your sleeping bag would sure come in handy again. It was just right when I borrowed it the last time—not too heavy, but warm at night.

SANDRA [modeling a response]: Jane, I don't mind you asking me, and I know you'll be disappointed, but I'd like you to realize that I have made this decision, based on my own needs, and I'd like you to try to understand. I really don't want to loan out my things any more—not even one more time.

JANE: O.K. I'm disappointed, because I need the sleeping bag, but I understand your decision.

During the group discussion the women pointed out that the leader, playing Sandra, had demonstrated an assertive response that was empathic but, unlike Sandra's first role play, was neither apologetic nor guilt-laden. The group agreed that this sounded effective, but thought that Jane might not have given up so easily, despite Sandra's assertiveness.

Role Play III

Then the leader asked Sandra to try again, to play herself this time, to speak in a firmer voice without apologizing, and to keep in mind her right to say *no*. The leader warned her that she would give her a hard time.

SANDRA [playing herself, taking a deep breath, and standing up straight]: Hi, Jane. Listen, I got your message about the camping trip, and I wanted to tell you about the sleeping bag—

JANE [played by leader, interrupting]: I'm so excited about this trip! I can't wait to go! You won't mind me borrowing your bag again, will you?

SANDRA: Sounds as if you'll have a good time on the trip. I realize my bag would be a help, but I want you to know that I've decided not to lend my camping equipment any more. [States what she wants directly.] It's getting worn out before its time.

JANE: Don't worry. I'll take good care of it. I always have in the past, haven't I?

SANDRA: Yes, you have, and I realize that. My decision certainly isn't based on anything you've done in the past. Since the bag is starting to wear out, I don't want to loan it any more. [Does not allow herself to get sidetracked. Sticks to the point and states what she wants directly.] I want to be able to use it myself . . . I wouldn't feel good about loaning it any more. [States what she is feeling.]

JANE [pushing even more]: Well . . . if that's how you feel, I'll just have to go along with your decision. But, Sandra, you *know* I've been counting on it [pleading voice], and it's such a bother to keep calling people to try to borrow all the equipment I need.

SANDRA: I can understand that you're not too happy with my decision [reflection of feelings], but I'd like you to realize my side of it too. I won't change my mind. I won't lend my camping equipment any more. [States what she wants.]

JANE [trying to produce guilt feelings]: If I can't borrow a bag I probably won't be able to go. [Implying that, if so, it will be Sandra's fault.]

SANDRA: Well, I do hope you get to go, but [repeats] I've told you my decision and [asserts herself about what's happening now] I really wish you'd stop pressuring me.

JANE [sighs]: Well, O.K.

Sandra told the group that she felt much better about her assertion this time than she had before. Then someone asked her how she would have felt if she had been pressured further. She said that she had realized that the pressure was manipulative, and had decided to stick to her point and tell Jane to stop pushing her. Everyone praised her for her directness, for letting Jane know that she understood Jane's situation and feelings, and for sticking to her initial decision even when Jane tried to push her. The session ended with Sandra making a commitment to the group that she would return Jane's phone call that very evening. She said she felt comfortable about making the call and realized that it was unlikely that her friend Jane would ever give her as hard a time as the leader had.

So this is how behavior rehearsal operates in an assertive training group with a leader. But it is possible to go through this procedure with a friend who understands the concepts of assertive behavior, and many of our group members continue to practice in this way with each other after the course has ended.

Making the Assertion
Appropriate to the Situation

After the first few weeks of assertive training, the women try out their assertions in real-life situations outside the groups and report back to us. Occasionally they tell us that the assertive statements they had made seemed to be overly harsh for the situation— they feel they came on too strong. As we have re-enacted the situation in role-play, we have seen that some of them did come on much stronger than the situation merited. Part of the practice in role-play, then, is devoted to assessing how strong the assertion needs to be in a given situation, and what would be an appropriate response.

For instance, if a salesperson tries to sell you a magazine subscription, you may consider whether you want it or not, decide that you don't, and then say, "Thank you for showing me what subscriptions are available, but I don't want to get any now." That may take care of it. However, if the salesperson persists, offering better bargains, more choices, and more pressure, you would then have to become stronger in your assertive refusal, saying, "I told you I wasn't interested in a magazine subscription. I'm not going to change my mind, and I want you to leave now."

Part of the assessment of each situation involves whether to assert or not. Another part of the assessment is to decide how strong an assertion is required, and how much emphasis it takes to be effective. The strength is not only in the choice of words, but also in how emphatic your voice and gestures are.

Gestalt: Empty Chair

One way to practice behavior rehearsal on your own is to role play both people in the conversation yourself. Play yourself as you sit facing an empty chair. Then get up and sit in the other chair when you play the other person, and respond. Switch chairs each time you switch roles. Anyone who happens to be watching might think you are crazy, but don't worry, it will give you an opportunity to consider both sides of the issue.

The following list of questions covers the main points that we've presented so far. It can also be a big help in developing your assertive behavior on your own.

Steps to Assertion: A Checklist

1. Clarify the situation and focus on the issue. What is my goal? What exactly do I want to accomplish?
2. How will assertive behavior on my part help me accomplish my goal?
3. What would I usually do to avoid asserting myself in this situation?
4. Why would I want to give that up and assert myself instead?
5. What might be stopping me from asserting myself?
   a. Am I holding on to irrational beliefs? If so, what are they?
   b. How can I replace these irrational beliefs with rational ones?
   c. Have I, as a woman, been taught to behave in ways that make it difficult for me to act assertively in the present situation? What ways? How can I overcome this?
   d. What are my rights in this situation? (State them clearly.) Do these rights justify turning my back on my conditioning?
6. Am I anxious about asserting myself? What techniques can I use to reduce my anxiety?

7. Have I done my homework? Do I have the information I need to go ahead and act?
8. Can I:
   a. let the other person know I hear and understand him/her?
   b. let the other person know how I feel?
   c. Tell him/her what I want?

This checklist provides a *thorough guide to all the steps to assertion*. We can refer to it and go through the whole process, or select the parts that will be helpful to us at the time. Of course, there are times when we can't refer to the checklist but must assert ourselves spontaneously or lose the opportunity.

As we work with the process more and more, we begin to integrate the steps, so that after a while we can quickly focus on the questions that have to do with the specific situation we're in. As we become comfortable with the assertive skills, we can then begin to use them efficiently in situations requiring quick responses.

In a follow-up meeting six weeks after the group sessions, Sheila told our group about her experiments in assertion. About a month ago she'd found a note in her mail box at the elementary school where she taught telling her that the school board was considering the elimination of all paid teacher aides in the elementary classrooms. She was very upset, because she had forty students and needed the aides to help her teach effectively.

She told her principal how she felt, and to her surprise he was very sympathetic. But what could be done? The principal said that he did not have the power to make the decisions, nor did he feel that he had much influence. "In my opinion," he said, "it would be better if you went directly to the board and presented a teacher's point of view."

To the group Sheila said, "Three months ago I would have either backed off completely or tried to get someone else to do it for me. This time, although I was nervous about it, I knew that I'd go ahead with it. I started to see it as a challenge.

"It was a perfect opportunity to use my checklist, and since this was the first time I was trying out an assertion without practicing with the group first, I wrote it all down."

Q: What is my goal for this assertion? What do I want to happen?

A: *The board will hear my arguments in favor of keeping teacher aides, and may decide to do so.*

Q: What would I do if I were not going to assert myself?

A: *I'd avoid the whole thing and end up complaining to other people if the aides left.*

Q: Why would I want to give up that (non-assertive) behavior?

A: *Because although I would avoid the anxiety of having to speak out, I know that I'll never get what I want unless I ask for it. Furthermore, from my own sense of integrity as a teacher, I feel a responsibility to speak out on matters that affect the quality of education.*

Q: What would stop me from expressing myself? Am I holding on to irrational beliefs?

A: *It's true, I am. I'm new in this district, and I keep thinking that the board members might be annoyed with me for speaking out at a time when the budget is tight. I'd feel awful if they got mad at me.*

Q: In what other ways might the board react?

A: *The board members might be interested in what I have to say.*

177

They might be happy to have new information.
They might already know what I will be telling them and be bored with me.
They might be annoyed at my taking up their time.
They might appreciate my concern with the quality of the elementary school education.
They might be totally indifferent to me.
They might appreciate hearing my case for what they wanted to do anyway, keep the teacher aides.

Even if they are annoyed at my "brashness," which I consider the worst outcome, I don't have to feel bad. I still will be doing what I want to do, and I can feel good about myself.

Q: Have I as a woman been taught to behave in ways that make it difficult for me to be assertive now? If so, how can I overcome these?

A: *I don't remember how or when I got this message, but I know that I grew up thinking that men should stand up for what they believe in, and that women should be quiet and support the men. No one ever told me that, but my father always did the talking and my mother kept quiet. It's what I saw. I can overcome this in two ways: by examining my attitudes, and by changing my behavior.*

Q: What are my rights in this situation?

A: *I have the right to express my opinion. It's something I want to do and I'll feel good about having done so. I also have the rights to be taken seriously and to be treated with respect.*

Q: Do these rights give me permission to turn my back on old messages?

A: *The right to express my opinion counteracts the message I have that women should not take stands or speak up. I'm going to give myself permission to speak to the board, based on my rights.*

Q: Am I anxious about behaving assertively? If so, what techniques can I use to reduce my anxiety?

A: *I was anxious (and still am, a little), but I already feel better because I've thought this through. I also know that I know how to listen attentively to the board's point of view. It gives me confidence to know I can rely on my skills.*

Also, just before I go in, I will take a few deep breaths, let them out slowly, and walk in standing straight. I can rehearse what I want to say, and this will help reduce my anxiety.

Q: Have I done my homework and gotten the information I need?

A: *I've read the minutes of the last four board meetings, and I've discussed the issues with my principal.*

Q: Can I now put together an assertive statement that reflects the three components of empathy, stating my feelings, and expressing my opinion?

A: *Yes. I can say: "I realize that the school board is feeling economic pressures right now and is trying to balance the budget. But I'm very upset about the possibility of eliminating teacher aides from the classroom. I would like you to hear what I have to say and to consider it seriously in making your decision." After that opening statement I can go on to list my objections and reasons.*

When Sheila finished telling the group what she had done with the checklist and how she had later presented her views to the board, she said she felt that the board had listened carefully, and that some of the members even appreciated her giving opinions. She felt that her assertion as an individual had served to open the door for possible future negotiations. She also realized that in this case it was going to take more than her individual assertion to influence board policy.

Buoyed up by the positive feelings she had from

179

having made her points, she was then in the process of getting the other teachers who agreed with her views to present a group statement to the board.

Although we have tended to emphasize individual skills, one of the outgrowths of assertive behavior can be the development of self-confidence, which can result in working with others to give our assertion collective power to bring about changes we believe in.

Exercises in Assertive Responses

I. Imagine yourself in the following situations, and practice asserting yourself, using the assertive model. Use the checklist, "Steps to Assertion," on pages 175–176 to help clarify your goals and overcome your blocks to assertion. Write down your assertive responses after each statement.

A. You and Jessica are co-workers in an office. Jessica asks you to give her a ride home every evening from now on. You don't want to do it. So you answer:

B. It's your lunch hour. You're sitting in a restaurant waiting for a friend. She breezes in a half hour late, sits down, and without any reference to her late arrival asks, "How are you?" You answer:

C. Just as you're about to go out the door, Anna calls you on the telephone. She starts to tell you about the problem she's been having with her parents. You're anxious to get off the phone. You say:

D. You're standing at the blouse counter. The saleswoman says, "Who's next?" It is your turn. The woman next to you says, "I am." You turn to her and . . .

E. You're at a community meeting. A man speaks up and urges the voters not to appropriate money for a day care center. He gives inaccurate information in his attempt to persuade people that there is no need for such a facility. You disagree with his ideas and his data. So you . . .

If these statements look familiar, it's because you read them in Chapter I. Now, turn back to pages 28–30 and check your answers with those we listed. Do your responses resemble our assertive ones? Remember, your answer doesn't have to be exactly the same as ours. We hope you were able to come up with assertive responses. If you still have difficulty formulating an assertive response, look over the examples again as a refresher.

More Exercises in Assertive Responses

Imagine yourself in the following situations and practice asserting yourself, using the assertive model. Use the checklist "Steps to Assertion" on pages 175–176 to help clarify your goals and overcome your blocks to assertion.

1. A close friend has taken you out to dinner, for a "special evening." You order your steak rare, and when you cut into it, it is medium. You don't want to put a damper on the evening, but you definitely prefer your steak rare. The waiter is heading toward your table. Rehearse what you would say now.

2. You bump into a friend who tells you that she's furious with you. She goes on and on about how angry she is, but never explains exactly why. She says: "Oh, come on, you know what I'm talking about. I've been upset all day just from thinking

181

about it. I'm so mad I don't even know if I can discuss it with you." Rehearse your response.

3. You are waiting in line to buy film tickets in advance. A stranger walks up to you and says, pleasantly, "I never thought the line would be this long, and I've got to keep an appointment in fifteen minutes. May I cut in ahead of you?" Rehearse your response.

4. The same situation as in 3, only this time the person wanting to cut in line is someone you know.

5. You are in the midst of preparing dinner. The telephone rings: It's a friend who starts the conversation with "I know this is a bad time to call you, but I have an important decision to make soon, and I just have to talk it over with someone." Rehearse your response.

6. You are in a taxi and you suspect that the driver is taking you on a roundabout route to your destination. Rehearse your assertion.

7. A friend of yours calls and gives you the name of a man she thinks you'd enjoy meeting. She suggests that you call him to make a date. You decide that you'd like to meet him. Rehearse your assertion.

8. You are sitting at a meeting and the person next to you is chain-smoking. Your eyes are tearing and you are very uncomfortable. Rehearse your assertion.

9. You have settled in for a quiet Sunday at home—the first in a long time. Your parents call and invite you over for the day. You don't want to go. Rehearse your assertion.

10. Your doctor gives you some medication for a recurring infection. When you ask him what the

medicine is for he says, "Oh, don't worry about it. Most of the girls are on this medication at one time or another. We'll call you if anything unusual shows up on the lab report." Rehearse your assertion.

11. You are in a dressing room at a department store. You have tried on several skirts and have just decided to buy one that you like a lot. The saleswoman comes in, and you hand her the skirt that you want and tell her you'll take it. She says, "Oh, honey. I really think the brown one is so much more becoming. You look like someone who appreciates quality. Believe me, even though the brown one costs more, it's worth it. The skirt you have here just doesn't compare to the other one. Try on the brown skirt again—I'm sure you'll change your mind." Rehearse your assertion.

12. You go to pick up your car at the service station, where you had left it for a lubrication and one new tire. When you arrive, the mechanic hands you the bill, which is twice as much as you had anticipated. When you question him he says: "Look, lady, the guy who worked on your car left. What can I tell you? He found something wrong with your carburetor, and you needed a tune up. Look, we're just trying to take care of your car. So let's settle up the bill now." Rehearse your assertion.

13. You work in an office. One day you hear from a co-worker that there is a position opening that you would like to have. You decide to tell the Personnel Manager that you want to be considered for the position. Rehearse your assertion.

14. You are ready to leave a party. As you start to

walk out the door, a man whom you know slightly puts his arm around you and says intently, "Don't go. You're the only reason I've stayed at this party. Come sit down with me. We have a lot to talk about." You are not interested in getting to know him any better than you already do. Rehearse your assertion.

15. You receive a notice informing you that your child has been placed in the classroom of a teacher whom you know to be notoriously incompetent. You decide to call the principal to ask to have your child switched to a different room. Rehearse your assertion.

16. You are a guest at a small party. Everyone is sitting around talking casually. The subject turns to women's issues. The host says, "Can you imagine? Now they're even writing books that teach women to be more assertive. I'm sure you'll agree—women are assertive enough already." You disagree. Rehearse your assertion.

17. You have had your apartment painted. As you begin moving the furniture back into place you notice that there is paint splattered all over the floor. You are angry. You decide to call the painter. Rehearse your assertion.

18. Your sister calls and she's angry. She's just had a fight with a mutual friend who is supposed to have coffee with you that day. Your sister wants you to hear her version of the fight, and you suspect that your friend will want you to hear her side, as well. You don't want to have to take sides. Rehearse your assertion.

19. You're handed a bill in a restaurant where you've had lunch with a friend. You add it up quickly and realize you've been overcharged. Your friend

says, "Oh well, let's just pay and not cause a scene," but you prefer to pay only what you owe. Rehearse your assertion.

20. A man in your office greets you every time he sees you with a leering comment on how good you look. He would probably claim he's paying you a compliment, but you want him to stop his personal remarks. Rehearse your assertion.

Evaluate Your Assertions

1. Did you say what you wanted to say?
2. Were you direct and unapologetic?
3. Did you stand up for your own rights without infringing on the rights of the other person?
4. Were you sitting or standing in an assertive posture?
5. Did your voice sound strong and calm? Were your gestures relaxed?
6. Did you feel good about yourself after you finished speaking?

We hope you have "YES" answers to most of these questions. Keep practicing your assertive responses until they feel comfortable to you.

Use the above list to help you evaluate your real life assertions too.

Putting It Together for Yourself

1. Choose some situations in your own life in which you would like to use assertive behavior. If you have kept a journal, refer to it when picking situations. It's important to begin with situations that don't cause a lot of anxiety and will have a good

chance of resulting in success. You can work your way up to tackling more difficult situations.

2. After you have chosen a specific situation, use the checklist presented in this chapter. Go through each step to analyze your current behavior, and how you can change it. Rehearse your assertion.

3. Now, you've put it together. It's time to apply it to *your* life. Go out and do it.

12

Sex Is Not a Dirty Word—
Let's Talk About It

MANY women think
that when a situation is intimate it is much more
difficult to talk honestly and be assertive. In sexual
relationships since the emotional stakes are high, your
anxiety may also increase. For many of us sexuality
is one of the last areas where we can be comfortable
with assertiveness, long after we've broken other
barriers.

The inhibitions on acknowledging and acting on our
sexual feelings are strong. They are often the result
of attitudes passed on over a lifetime. These messages
may have been given by parents or other adults during
our childhood and adolescent years. In many homes,
girls are told that masturbation is bad; sex is dirty;
sex is painful; sex is done *to* or *for* you (rather than *by*
or *with* you); sex is shameful; you should save sex for
marriage or men won't respect you; if you enjoy sex
you should feel guilty. The paradoxical message is:
"Sex is dirty—save it for the one you love!"

In addition to direct and indirect messages about
sex, the strongest message of all may be "Don't discuss
sex. It's taboo." Often a dry lecture explaining the
facts of menstruation and the "facts of life," duly
delivered in a guarded manner, is a parent's only
reference to sex in the presence of the child. This itself

can convey the message that sex is a forbidden topic of conversation.

If as children we have learned that sex is a taboo subject, how does this affect the way we express our sexual needs as adults? We asked four women with different life styles to meet with us and talk about assertiveness in their own sex lives. Dr. Beverly Hotchner, Executive Director of the Center for Human Concerns, a sexuality resource center in St. Louis, Missouri, joined us too. The women were:

Bev Hotchner, forty-five, married twenty-three years, with two grown sons.

Amanda, twenty-two, unmarried, dating, feminist graduate student.

Lilly, thirty-five, recently divorced mother of a small child, commercial artist.

Marie, fifty, married thirty years to a businessman, housewife, mother of two grown children and a teen-ager, active in community service.

Sandy, twenty-six, manager of a bookstore, living with a graduate student.

This is what they said:

BEV: It's important to help women to become aware of what they do to stop themselves from being assertive in sexual relationships. Most women think something else stops them.

MARIE: That's not just women, that's people.

BEV: Sure, that applies to both sexes, but tonight we're talking about women.

AMANDA: Well, if we do stop ourselves, what makes it so hard for us to be assertive in sex?

BEV: The obvious things stop us. Most women complain of embarrassment: "I could never say that in front of him, never in a million years. I can hardly say it to myself."

Or women feel vulnerable: "If I say that, I'd be open to all kinds of problems—rejection, put-downs, being laughed at. I couldn't stand that treatment. I'm already too nervous about the subject anyway." A classic irrational belief: "I couldn't stand that."

Other women fear that if they said what they want they'd be seen as excessively demanding, promiscuous. They're afraid that they won't get what they want anyway, that men will see them as threatening and be turned off.

LILLY: That all sounds more familiar than I'd like to admit. I can see how I stop myself, especially when sex isn't satisfying and yet I can't tell my partner. I'm afraid that he might think I don't like him well enough, or that I'm insatiable . . .

AMANDA: Or that I'm not doing something right.

BEV: Or that I'm just a nagging wife, and this is one more hassle in a long series.

LILLY: Or I'm just trying to put him down.

MARIE: That was my biggest problem. If there was one area in which my husband and I could communicate both verbally and non-verbally, it was sex. For years that got us over some of the other rough spots that we couldn't talk about. It worked that way until we started having sex problems. Then I couldn't tell Bob what I was thinking for fear of hurting him.

BEV: Our conditioning leads men to believe that they are supposed to be the teachers and the authorities about sex. If we dare to express what we want and it's an idea that's new to them, many

189

men feel their virility is being threatened. That's partly why it's so hard for men and women to talk about sex.

AMANDA: I know that I've often thought, "If he really loved me he'd know what I want. He shouldn't have to ask—and neither should I." How irrational!

BEV: This view feeds the myth that sex should be natural and spontaneous and beautiful and perfect! We shouldn't have to talk about it or work at it.

AMANDA: For me the myth is somewhat different. I never really had any sexual experience until now. Since I'm a feminist and labeled a heavy Women's Libber, I feel that I should know everything about sex, and I'm embarrassed because I don't. My self-consciousness stops me from saying what I want or asking the questions I need to. I just don't take the responsibility for what I'm feeling.

SANDY: Your embarrassment just shows that a lot of the sexual revolution is a myth. The idea that now we're supposed to know everything—and have ten orgasms in a row—is just one more thing for women to live up to.

AMANDA: Yes. And I don't like the idea of being taught by a man. But I've got to learn somehow. [Laughter.] So I set myself up to depend on what he knows, and I'm afraid he'll think I'm weird if I ask him to do anything he's not doing.

MARIE: What would you like him to do?

AMANDA: Well, mostly I'd just like to be able to talk more about the whole thing. But during sex I start to get scared, and then I tune out. Then I really get angry at myself for not enjoying it.

LILLY: I know what you mean. During the first ten

190

years of my marriage I didn't even know that sex should be good. I thought that everyone who went on about how great it could be was exaggerating. I didn't realize that either of us should know anything more.

BEV: It's very important to be clear about what you want. Most of the women who come to my sexuality workshops don't know what to ask for. They haven't explored their bodies or given themselves permission to find out what feels good, and so they don't know what they like. Before they can ask for what they want, they may have to discover what pleases them.

SANDY: I think it is hard for women to feel free to explore themselves. Although it's the logical first step, it tends to go against what we've been taught. It's easier to put the responsibility on someone else.

BEV: Easier to let somebody explore her body for her?

SANDY: Sure. We've been taught "hands off."

BEV: Well, that's true, but many women feel more comfortable about exploring their own bodies rather than letting someone else do it.

LILY: I think I know my own body pretty well, but when I'm with a man it's still very hard for me to say what I want, even though I know what feels good. If I don't like something all I do is tell him that. This frustrates a man, because he wants to know, "Well, what *do* you want?"

BEV: So you're able to give general negative reactions —"I don't like that"—but you don't go on to the positive.

SANDY: Me too. I can immediately react on a gut level and say "No" or "That hurts" or "Stop it." But

191

then either I don't feel the need to be more specific, or I don't want to have to get intellectual and to think any more.

LILLY: I know what you mean about not wanting to get into the mind thing when you're having sex. Sometimes, after the fact, I've tried to think and talk about what I liked and what I didn't when we last made love.

SANDY: How did that work?

LILLY: O.K., but talking about sex is still difficult for me. I'm non-assertive in a lot of situations, and my difficulty with sexual discussion is part of the larger problem.

SANDY: Have you ever told your partner of your fears of discussing sex?

LILLY: Well, a little. I told him I was afraid I'd hurt his feelings. He said, "I'll be responsible for myself. It's more unfair to me if you don't say what you want." Maybe I should start by telling him how uncomfortable I am talking about sex.

BEV: That triggers something. We usually think of assertiveness as a verbal skill. But with sex, assertiveness is action as well. It is doing what feels right, whether it's movement or breathing or position or getting the right kinds of stimulation. It's being assertive enough to be satisfied. And it may not be verbal at all.

MARIE: Through most of my marriage Bob and I did communicate easily about sex. We did talk a lot about what we needed. We made sounds— "Mmmm," when something was good. Or movements that said, "Wonderful." Sometimes we'd lie in bed afterward and talk about what was really great for us, or what one of us had liked but not the other.

If one of us wanted to try something new we'd stop only if the other might be physically hurt. Some of the explorations were mostly talk: "This is what I'd like to do. How do you feel about it?" This way we'd be able to find out how the other might react.

BEV: That's very good. You sound very healthy sexually.

MARIE: Yes, our sex life was great. But when I went through menopause I got so uptight that some of the things that used to be stimulating didn't work any more. I think that was *my* problem, because it wasn't that way with my friends. I'd always prided myself on enjoying sex and on being good in bed, but when that started going bad I was really scared. It had been easy to talk when our sex life was good, but when it wasn't I clammed up.

Poor Bob was vulnerable too, and didn't know what was wrong. Here was territory he thought he knew very well, but now it was changing. We didn't talk about it, but I was frustrated too. I can remember waking up one sunny day and thinking, "Life just isn't as much fun any more."

AMANDA: That's hard. What did you do?

MARIE: I said to myself, "If the next thirty years are like this . . . my God! What am I going to do?" I knew I couldn't live this way any more.

I talked about this in my assertive training group. Then I went home and told Bob I had something serious to talk about. I realized that even though our conversation would be difficult, our silence was hurting each other more. And there was a lot at stake for me.

We set aside a special time to talk when we wouldn't be interrupted, and it was hard in the beginning. Once we really got to discussing what we both wanted, what might work, what we wanted to try . . . Well, we talked for hours and that led us to bed and . . . Wow! It was really worth it!

That broke the barrier, and since then we're back to normal and sex is great.

SANDY: That sounds terrific.

BEV: Lilly, I'm wondering whether you've run into any new kinds of problems since your divorce.

LILLY: Well, of course there's the old cliché about the divorced woman whom men assume is sex-starved and figure, "She'll go to bed with me because there's no reason not to. It won't hurt anybody." I quickly learned to feel comfortable saying "No" when I didn't want to.

I have a much harder time, though, taking the initiative with men. Suddenly I'm totally responsible for my social and sexual life. If no one is breaking down my door, then sometimes I have to take the lead, and that's not been easy. Sometimes I've suggested to men I've met at parties that it might be fun to see each other again.

MARIE: That's great!

LILLY: Yes, but inside I'm very shaky if I think they might say "No." I have to keep reminding myself that I have the right to do this—and that they have the right to turn me down.

AMANDA: I've been bothered for a long time because I don't assert myself. Once I decided to try hard to be assertive with my boyfriend. I said, "This is uncomfortable for me to discuss, but sometimes I feel as if you're in control of our whole sexual relationship. We always make love when *you*

194

feel like it." He's a morning person and I'm a night person. So he falls asleep on me at night and wakes me up in the morning when I want to sleep.

So he listened understandingly, but the next time we made love he was very passive. I wasn't sure why, and I didn't ask. I was scared, but I didn't know what I was supposed to do. I was more concerned with whether I was making love right than with really enjoying it.

When we finished he said, "Well, this time I let you have the control. How did you feel?" I had hated it, but I didn't tell him that.

BEV: Why did you hate it?

AMANDA: I don't like being in control, and I wanted to tell him that *neither* of us needs to control the other.

And I was unhappy because I was afraid to talk about it, even afterwards. I was mad at myself, because I should have said something. Even though we trust each other, he's shy too. I know my reaction was irrational, but both of us are inhibited when it comes to talking about sex.

BEV: Your communication outside the bedroom is pretty good?

AMANDA: Yes.

BEV: Usually that transfers pretty well. Not always, but often when communication is poor in general it carries over to the bedroom, where people are even more vulnerable.

MARIE: Amanda, in some way this image of being an assertive woman seems to be a real burden to you. You started out by asserting yourself, telling him you didn't like him to be in control. But you didn't

195

follow that up with what you wanted and how you felt. And finally you got angry at yourself for not being assertive.

AMANDA: Yes, I think I'm falling into a new set of "shoulds" and "oughts." I'm the one who's making assertiveness a burden by feeling I either have to be totally assertive or else, blah, I'm a failure.

BEV: That leaves you with two kinds of discomfort to deal with. Now you're not just dissatisfied with sex, but also with yourself for not always being assertive about it.

AMANDA: O.K. I can see that I trade one rigid set of rules for another. It's a trap, another impossible standard to try to live up to. I do want to be more assertive sexually, but I don't have to berate myself each time I don't measure up to some ideal of assertive perfection.

SANDY: My own experience of not communicating during sex is a lot like Amanda's; I get the feeling that I'm alone in a crowd. Although there's supposed to be this great sharing, it ends up as my personal, lonesome pastime, even though another person happens to be there. So it's a double disappointment. It's *my* sex, not *ours*. Perhaps there's physical satisfaction, but that's all.

BEV: Yet at some point it has to be *your* sex for your own sake or you don't have much pleasure. That doesn't tune out the other person or destroy the beauty of the relationship. You also need to focus on your own sensations in order to experience pleasure.

SANDY: I realize that. But the traditional ideal is perfect communication. If I'm not communicating, then that doesn't fit my ideal.

BEV: But you're non-verbally communicating your enjoyment, and the other person should be picking that up and getting turned on by it.

SANDY: Oh sure, if it's going that way. But Amanda was talking about keeping quiet when you need to talk about something you don't like. Sex can continue through that, but it's lonely.

LILLY: When you need to communicate and you don't, you either put up a barrier or you back off.

MARIE: You seem to be saying that every time you have sex you expect perfection. That's not possible. There are varying degrees. Perhaps one of you gets distracted, say by a noise outside, while the other person isn't affected. The partner has the right to be satisfied.

But sex does not have to be a magnificent experience for both people every single time. If you have less rigid expectations, then you can be more relaxed. You don't have to be paranoid and start questioning the whole relationship each time sex is slightly less than perfect.

LILLY: That's true. But afterwards you could say, "That wasn't as good for me as it could have been." Or "I wish this would have happened." Somehow to at least be able to talk about it would be a help.

AMANDA: Is it any easier for you to talk about the positive?

LILLY: Yes. I want us to discuss what we enjoyed and why, so we'll know what to do again.

BEV: In my experience it's much more uncomfortable for some people to say what's good than to talk about what's not.

AMANDA: Or we give praise in a general way—"Gee, that was neat"—instead of in specifics, especially about sex.

BEV: I like to teach people to say "Yes" as much as

possible. There are very few times when you have to say "No." There are alternatives. Like when the guy says, "I'm horny tonight," and she says, "I've had a terrible day and I'm tired. How about taking a shower together tonight, instead?" He might or might not go along with that. He could say, "Well, I'd rather not. How about rubbing my back or something?" That way nobody has to be disappointed, and everybody gets a little pleasure. It's simple, but it works.

SANDY: That expression "taking responsibility for your own pleasure" sounds so easy when *you say* it.

BEV: But, it's a foreign concept for most of us.

AMANDA: I'm beginning to realize that—and this may sound naive—but sex would be so much better if I did ask for it. It seems so much sexier to know what you want and to ask for it. Making love that way would be wonderful!

MARIE: That's different from thinking that you have to know all the answers or always say the right things. Just let yourself go a little.

AMANDA: Imagine making love knowing and asking for what you wanted. That would really heighten the experience.

SANDY: Yes. I'm ready to go home and try it!

LILLY: I have to admit that even though I was pleased when you asked me to come here tonight to talk about assertiveness and sex, I was also nervous. Even with a group of women, those old taboos about discussing sex were still there. But I'm glad I came. The discussion has given me a lot to think about.

Social conditioning has taught children of both sexes that sex is a taboo topic. This powerful restriction carries over to adulthood, influencing both sexual communication and behavior, either inhibiting the partners from discussing sex or creating considerable embarrassment if they do try to talk. Moreover, many women, having learned to be passive and to let men take the lead, are extremely reserved in sexual matters. This is as true of feminists who came of age in the '70s as it of their mothers.

Thus, women may be reticent about making requests of their partner, either negative ("Stop it. That hurts.") or positive ("That was marvelous. Do it again!") or neutral ("How would it be if we tried . . . ?"). And when women do talk, they may be too embarrassed to deal in specifics; only the vague generalities are safe.

Some of the inhibitions to sexual assertiveness are the result of irrational beliefs. Women are often inhibited by the assumption that if they make requests or initiate behavior they'll be rejected, or laughed at. Women also hold the equally mistaken assumption that an assertive woman is less appealing than a passive one.

Taboos, irrational beliefs, and myths also contribute to problems in communication about sex. Although assertiveness may not resolve all our sex problems, it can create a climate for more open communication. It can also help us realize that we can take some responsibility for getting what we want, instead of waiting for our partner to sense our sexual needs. Assertiveness can help us communicate honestly; it can help us risk a new kind of communication rather than suffer—or permit our partner to suffer—in silence.

As Dr. Hotchner has observed, "When a woman becomes assertive and takes charge of her life, she feels more confident. As a result, her feelings about her sexuality are enhanced and her relationships are more pleasurable. Assertiveness in sexuality often transfers to other areas of her life. Then communication in general improves and at the same time sex becomes mutual, rather than male-dominated."

Whenever women decide to become assertive, in sex as well as in other areas of life, it's acting on that decision that ultimately counts.

13

Back to School, Back to Work

From the Feminine Mystique to the Feminist Mystique

WHAT happens to the woman brought up on the Cinderella story who expects to live happily ever after? Until recently she appeared as Supermom in the women's magazines, TV commercials, and family situation comedies. Supermom was stage center. She was perpetually active and energetic, with gleaming hair and floors to match. Her life revolved around her beautiful children and a loving husband who came home to a picture-book domestic scene of piping-hot dinner, immaculate house, and harmonious family.

For years Supermom was instructed in her role by her own family and the popular literature of the day. She was bombarded with advice about clever interior decorating, imaginative birthday parties for children, and lavish dinners complete with crown roast and candlelight. And if, perchance, her roasts were a bit overdone, or the children squabbled at the dinner table, or her homemade cape with color-coordinated scarf didn't capture the glamour of the illustration on the pattern package, she was left with the sinking feeling that she wasn't quite measuring up.

Nevertheless, through all her efforts she was expected to be smiling, happy, contented, fulfilled. If she had moments of self-doubt, she probably kept them to herself. After all, how could anyone as fortunate as she be dissatisfied? And if she did risk voicing her discontent, she was likely to be told how to organize her time better, or she was made to feel guilty for her failure to accept the responsibilities of mature womanhood. If she realized that something was not quite right with her world, whether she said so or not, she felt alone, a misfit for having these feelings.

We may be telling ourselves that we've come a long way since those days of idealized Supermom. Since the explosion of the feminine mystique, women have taken a closer look at the tyranny of that model of perfection. And now our newspapers are filled with articles about the new woman: the brilliant mother of three who has been elected to the board of Conglomerate America; the new young legislator who keeps her baby in a playpen at the statehouse. Television brings us the gay divorcee, super competent at home and on the job, with well-adjusted, adoring children and a variety of men to provide love and comic relief. Even commercials portray this new image, as Mother, a Ph.D. in biochemistry, whips into the house from her job at the lab to provide her glowing children with a nutritious drink, which they gulp down with gratitude.

Of course. These are the heroines of the Feminist Mystique. Supermom has not been replaced, but on her beaming image has been imposed that of Ms. Superwoman, the super competent—still smiling, still running an immaculate household with one hand while with the other she (almost) rules the world. The stereotypes of one mystique have led to the dictates of another. Whereas women used to be asked at parties, "How many children do you have?" the new question is "What do you do?" The former assumed that the woman was fully occupied with her motherhood; the latter presumes that she has a job or a profession. In fact, the answer "I stay at home" or "I'm just a housewife" is often uttered apologetically, and may be received with a cool "Oh," followed by strained silence.

The woman caught in a mystique, be it feminine or feminist, is boxed in by externally imposed expectations. Today's woman may run on the treadmill faster and faster, trying to be all things to all people, yet still feeling inadequate, still not quite measuring up. Certainly this image of the new woman is far removed from the true spirit of feminism, which aims to enable every woman to develop according to her own needs and to find fulfillment on her own terms.

Assertive skills can help break the repressive molds of both mystiques. They can help a woman to define herself, to claim the power to be her own person instead of Supermom or Superwoman. When she truly believes she has rights, and develops the ability to exercise them, she can grow beyond the limitations that both the feminine and the feminist mystiques impose.

Women today are often seeking a new definition, especially when they reach their middle years and realize that their children are growing up and away. Whether or not they were ever Supermoms, they find themselves outgrowing their principal role as mother. At this point they may begin to take a long look at themselves, to identify who they've been, who they are, and what they want for the remaining years of their lives. This is the time of transition and preparation for another role, not necessarily that of Superwoman, but very likely one of student or wage earner.

Whether or not we wanted to be in the traditional female roles of wife and mother, if that's all we have been prepared for the decision to change may be either threatening or exciting—or a little of both. If our sensitivity, passivity, and nurturing abilities have been developed at the expense of other qualities, we may feel stuck with our familiar roles. We may be afraid to leave the safe for the challenging. This is the time we may need to examine ways of developing new confidence and assertiveness.

Deciding to change can present problems. Sometimes even if we have learned to rely on ourselves as Supermoms we may need an assertive push to transfer our abilities to a college classroom or to a job.

Assertive training can help provide that push. It can help the woman in transition become more self-reliant and begin to realize "I have rights of my own. I count." And it can help her develop specific skills to use in her new environment.

Deciding to Make the Transition: Using Assertive Skills to Help You Get There

---

The skills acquired in assertive training can be invaluable to a woman who is in the process of deciding to make some changes in her life. In particular, assertive skills can help her handle a job or classroom situation, solve the logistical problems in making the change, and face the possible negative reactions of others.

The propaganda that "life begins at forty" may have a hollow ring for women poring over college catalogs, want ads, or job descriptions. "How can I possibly do it? Things are so much more complicated now than they were when I graduated from high school. I'll never be able to master all those details." "I've been away from studying for twenty years. Today's college kids know so much more than we did! And the competition is so stiff. How can I keep up with them?" "Who would want to hire me if they could get some young thing?" "It takes every minute of my day just to keep the household running. How could I possibly take on anything else?" "My typing and shorthand are rusty." "I didn't do very well when I was in school before. Why should I expect to do any better the second time around?"

These characteristic self-doubts could stop some of us cold. Assertive training can help us look at these doubts and figure out whether or not they are irrational—and, if they are, it can help us act on the reality. Many of these beliefs probably are irrational if they focus on one fear and fail to examine other factors, such as:

- Academic competition depends on specific institutions, classes, and instructors. We can investigate these for ourselves.
- Are we discounting our years away from school or paid employment as having been wasted? Are we ignoring the experience we've gained in managing a family, running a household, and volunteer activities? Some people compare a well-run household with a well-run corporation. It's something to think about.

205

- Although we may have added demands if we return to school or to work, we are free of some of the pressures on younger students or workers, who are coping with living on their own, or with a new marriage or a new baby. Even if the reality *is* that we're older and out of practice, we can use assertive skills to help us move toward our new goals.

Part of the process of overcoming self-doubts is starting to polish up old abilities, and before you know it, self-doubts are likely to be replaced with self-confidence. Being assertive can help us decide to go back to school or work. It can help us to find out about courses in reading and work improvement as preparation for this. And assertiveness can help us exercise our rights to find out what our qualifications must be, what will be expected of us, or how we apply for a scholarship if we are eligible.

Solving Logistical Problems

Assertiveness may also help us to deal with the logistics of juggling family, home, and the new role without going under. Although new demands added to our already hefty responsibilities will require adjustments, we don't need to make them all by ourselves.

For instance, in juggling arrangements for child care, social schedules, classes, and car pools, most of us can use help from our friends and families, though we may have to be assertive to get it.

- We can ask them for cooperation—to take over some of the responsibilities for us.
- We can learn to say *no* to taxing requests from others.
- We can find out about professional services to help

keep things running smoothly, such as child-care agencies and car pools and day camps.

Facing Others' Negative Reactions:

It may take considerable assertiveness to cope with others' negative reactions when we announce our decision to return to school or to work. Some of the following reactions may sound familiar:

1. "Being a wife and mother is the most important thing a woman can do, but it takes full-time to do it right."
2. "I don't see why you have to go to school to fulfill yourself. Why can't you find other things to keep busy without hassling your family?"
3. "What right do you have to go out and take a job away from a man who needs it to support his family, especially in this tight job market? After all, your husband's earning a decent living."
4. "How can you possibly go off and leave your children?"
5. "Some of my other friends went back to work, and frankly, once they did I could never stay really friendly with them. They just weren't the same people any more."
6. "I don't mind your taking classes as long as it isn't too big a deal. I don't want to have to do any more work around here, though. After all, I'm the one who's bringing in the money."

Some of these statements could be openings for an argument, particularly if the speaker is threatened by our decision. Yet a good assertive response can open the way for communication and perhaps even defuse an argument. We can let the other person

207

know we've heard him, and then state what we feel. Here is how some women have handled these questions.

1. "Yes, being a wife and mother is very important, but so is my work. We may have to live with more dust on the floor and fewer gourmet meals, but that's still what's best for me, and it won't hurt the rest of the family."

2. "I know you're concerned about my family, and so am I. We're working out ways to share responsibilities, because I've reached a point in my life where I need the structure of school—and eventually of a job."

3. "I agree that families need support, especially in this job crunch. But the point is that I'm trained for that job, I have as much right to it as anyone else with the same qualifications, and I want to try to get it."

4. "That's a reasonable question. I have a good co-op nursery school for them in the morning, and Dan will be able to help some in the afternoons. The children will be fine—and we really need the extra money I'll earn."

5. "Thanks for letting me know you're worried. I think if we both want to keep on being friends we can work it out. It's worth an effort that I'm willing to make. Are you?"

6. "Yes, and you're a good provider. But I'm entitled to some satisfactions on my own, too. Besides, extra study now might help me to get a job later on—and that could take some of the pressure off you."

Even if our answer doesn't change anyone's mind, we can feel better about ourselves for having stated our point of view honestly, and we can also acknowledge the other person's right to his or her opinion. Assertive training helps us express ourselves directly, without becoming defensive. It also helps us realize that we have rights, as wives, as mothers, as people—including those of setting priorities, of being taken seriously, and of not being responsible for others' negative reactions to our decisions.

Assertive Training and the World of Work

The first step in finding a job is deciding what we want to do and then exploring the available possibilities. Jobs rarely come to us if we sit back and wait for them to drop into our laps. We need to find out everything we can, to talk to people working in fields that interest us, tell everyone we know that we're looking for a job, ask questions, and read want ads everywhere—and ask more questions.

The first stages of job exploration can be slow and frustrating. We may need to remind ourselves of our rights, and to take another look at the irrational beliefs which may be holding us back. We have the right to make requests—for information and appointments. Others have the right to say *no;* if we're imposing, it's their responsibility to tell us so. We can stop worrying about whether we're bothering people or asking dumb questions; if we are, they'll tell us (assuming that they're sufficiently assertive).

The next stage of job hunting is the interviews. When we asked the personnel manager of a large corporation whether she thought assertiveness was important for the working woman, she said, "As a recruiter, I'm constantly on the lookout for assertive people. Our firm doesn't hire people in sales and management unless they're assertive." Initiating a handshake, asking questions, speaking up on one's own behalf, negotiating salary—all these components of the job interview call for assertion.

We may want to practice relaxation exercises before the interview, or rehearse questions—and answers to possible questions—with a friend. We have the right to request information about the job: its hours, duties, salary, fringe benefits, opportunities for advancement. The personnel manager quoted above told us that she was horrified when she offered a job to a woman who accepted it without even inquiring about the salary.

In one of our assertive training groups, recently, Olivia, a political pollster, with a graduate degree in public affairs, told us how she assertively tried to find a job for herself when she and her husband left Washington and moved to the midwest. Olivia had been the chief pollster for a Presidential candidate in the last campaign, and had definite ideas about how her skills would be valuable to corporations.

So she made an appointment to see Mr. Kohlman, the president of the largest public relations firm in her new city. She explained what kind of work she wanted to do and said, "I don't think you realize that your firm needs me. But I believe it does, and I'd like you to give me an opportunity to prove it."

Mr. Kohlman listened and decided to give her the chance to do freelance work for the company. Olivia's assertiveness had paid off. She had gotten her foot in the door.

Once she started taking on freelance jobs for the

firm, she kept in touch with the president to make sure that he was aware of the value of her work. After six months of steady freelance work, Olivia went to see Mr. Kohlman once again. This time she said, "You've seen what I can do, and you've told me that you're pleased with my work. I appreciate having had the chance to freelance, but now I'd like a full-time job." Olivia told us that she had been anxious about being so direct, but once again her assertiveness paid off. She was offered a job and a chance to build her own department.

During the past two years her staff has grown to include five full-time employees and eighty part-time interviewers. Recently Olivia's department became a separate corporation, a subsidiary of the parent company, and Olivia, at age 28, is its president.

We heard an equally encouraging story from Joan, age 39, a lawyer who had been an assistant attorney general for a year. Her problem started when a new attorney general was elected and, the word quickly got around that he would be bringing in some of his own staff. Since Joan was low in seniority, her job was in jeopardy. The other low seniority attorney, a man, started looking for a new job right after the election.

Joan, however, was not content to accept political tradition when it meant the loss of her job, and prepared to confront her new boss. She got letters commending her work from some of the state agencies she had served. With these in hand, she made an appointment to see the new attorney general, opening the conversation with, "I'd like to tell you why it's a mistake to let me go. Let me show you what I've accomplished in the last year, and what I'd like to do in the next four." She then elaborated upon her accomplishments, without being defensive and without putting down any of her colleagues.

The attorney general heard her out, without indicating his reaction. Within a few days she was notified that she would be retained. Some months later her boss told her that he'd been impressed with her thoughtful, direct presentation and her desire to move forward with her work. Because of this he decided not to replace her. Through her assertive act she had kept her job.

Once we get the job, assertiveness can help us get along with the people around us. At times we may have to refuse unreasonable requests; the alternative is to take on too much and end up doing nothing very well. An experienced executive secretary suggested the following assertive solution to the problem of being asked to do an unreasonble amount of work: "I know there's a lot to be done, Mr. Fields, but I'm overloaded right now. Tell me what your top priorities are and I'll get to work on those first."

We may also need to assert ourselves by making requests: for a raise, for time off, for a change in duties, for a promotion, for equipment or information. We may need to assert our rights, such as the right to be taken seriously. When the boss of a woman executive introduced her at a board meeting as "the prettiest district manager I've got," she replied, "I don't want to be the prettiest, I'd rather be the best." As we move up in status or power and have people who work for us, we may need to assert ourselves by being open and direct with the people who work for us, and by encouraging them to be the same.

Rita had recently been promoted to a supervisory position in an engineering firm. Within the first two months she realized that she was going to have to talk to John, an engineer who was chronically late—both to work and in turning in projects. Since John had been an unsuccessful candidate for Rita's new position, criticizing him would be particularly difficult.

Before she talked to John, she went through parts of the checklist on pages 181–182. She began bolstering herself by recognizing that her job gave her not only the right but the responsibility to tell John to be on time. She saw that by being non-assertive, or by asserting herself ineffectively, she would lose her own self respect and the respect of her co-workers. She also knew that she didn't want to make an enemy of a person who was valuable to the firm, and whom she would be working with for some time to come. So she decided to talk to John with these goals in mind:

1. My discussion will deal specifically with John's late projects and late arrival at work.
2. I will listen carefully to him and try to understand what he's saying and how he feels. I'll let him know I've heard and understood.
3. I will let him know how I feel about him; I value him as a person, I like the quality of his work, and I enjoy working with him. I may tell him that I don't relish the need for this particular discussion, but . . .
4. I will be firm in telling him what I want him to do.

Rita told us that merely setting goals and believing that she would be able to communicate them assertively made it easier for her to do it. The results were even better than she'd hoped for. She'd had a good talk with John and felt that his respect for her had increased. And, she was starting to feel better about her own abilities to handle her new job.

Roslyn, a college administrator recently described what happened when she became the first and only woman on the executive faculty committee. "I kept coming up with what I thought were pretty good ideas," she said. "But I started to notice that as soon as I'd had my say, the men continued to talk as if I had never spoken, and I assumed it was because my ideas were not very good.

"But then I realized that often one of the men would say exactly what I'd just said, perhaps in slightly different words, and it would be heralded as the solution. The committee would be quick to appreciate the man.

"I'd go home to my husband and say, 'You know, I think I have a communication problem.' But gradually I realized that the problem was not in my communication, but that the men in the meeting had trouble hearing anything from a head that happened to be attached to a body wearing a skirt.

"I decided that if I wanted to have any influence on the committee I needed to be recognized for my contributions. At the next meeting, I spoke up and said, 'Gentlemen, during the meeting today I made two suggestions that no one paid much attention to. Later they were re-worded by someone else, and this time they were received enthusiastically. I would like to point this out since it has happened before, and it is bothering me.'"

Roslyn told us that the men on the committee seemed a little taken aback by her assertiveness, but they did agree that the suggestions that day were re-worded versions of what she had first said. In the very next meeting Roslyn noticed that the men paid attention to everything she said and she began to feel that she was being accepted as an equal.

The working women who have talked to us about assertiveness remind us that it is also necessary to assess risks when we want to assert. You may not want to ask for an extra week's vacation (even though you want it) if you know that the last person who did so was fired. Sometimes the risks of asserting yourself are just too great, and you have to evaluate this for yourself. But even within the limits imposed by the power structure, you usually increase your own power many times if you are asser-tive rather than non-assertive. The more assertive you are, the more self-confident and responsible you be-come, and the more successful you're likely to be.

Conclusion

Briefly, the process of making the transition from wife and mother to student or wage earner is as follows:

1. Understand your own attitudes about your pres-ent roles and the new one you are thinking of taking on. What are your goals (short- and long-term)? What do you want to be like five and ten years from now and for the rest of your life? Will going back to school or back to work (or both) help you fulfill these?

2. Figure out whether or not your expectations are realistic. This can be done by getting all the informa-tion you can about the prospective jobs or schools.

3. Polish up your rusty talents. Prepare your family and friends for the transition by talking about how

they feel about your decision, and by working out new schedules for car pools, household tasks, and the like.

4. Be assertive and do it! Enroll in the courses; look for the job.

5. Stick by your decision. Doubts, difficulties in scheduling, extra pressures on the family, unanticipated problems are likely to occur, no matter how thorough your advance planning has been. It may seem easier at times to give up. But before making such a dramatic decision, consider the alternatives. What do you *really* want? And what are you willing to do to get—and keep—it?

Assertiveness can help you make your own choices and figure out who you are and who you want to be. And assertive training can help you develop the skills and strength to be not the Supermom or Superwoman of the feminine and feminist mystiques, but your own person.

14

You Can Do It

WE believe in assertive behavior. We've seen many women use it and start to take control of their own lives. We've watched them grow and support each other. We're excited by what we've seen, and the members of our assertive training groups share our enthusiasm. They have started to do things they never thought they could before, and they are learning to be more comfortable with themselves and with others.

Becoming assertive is an ongoing process. Part of that process is building an awareness of your rights, your blocks, and your own patterns of behavior. It is also a process of practicing new skills. Becoming comfortable with these skills may take time—but remember, you have the right to make mistakes! Keep trying out your assertive behavior and give yourself a chance to improve.

Our experience and the experiences of the women in our groups have been that we feel good about ourselves when we act assertively. Assertive behavior is not a panacea. But assertive behavior can help us to communicate better, to improve our relationships, to satisfy our needs, and to like ourselves more. Assertion leads to self-confidence, and self-confidence leads to more assertion.

Once women learn to be assertive, they have a skill that will give them more choices, more independence, more strength, and more control over their own lives.

It's worked for many women.

We hope it works for you.

Appendix

In our attempt to evaluate the effects of the assertive training procedures used in our classes in assertive training at the University of Missouri–St. Louis Extension Division, we sent follow-up questionnaires to 130 women who had been in our groups. Ninety-four returned the questionnaire.

Among the many interesting findings, we noted that 95% of the women said that in the 6 to 18 months since they had finished the course, they were able to maintain or increase the level of assertive skills they had achieved by the end of the six-week session.

Over 90% said they could adapt their skills to completely novel situations or to new situations similar to those worked on in the training sessions.

Of the 85% of the respondents who said they experienced some changes in their lives as a result of assertive training, three-quarters of them felt that they had played an *active* role in bringing about those changes.

This analysis is subject to the limitations inherent in self-assessment studies, but can serve as a beginning for further evaluation. It will be reported on in greater detail in Michael Mayo, Martin Bloom, and Joan Pearlman, "Effectiveness of Assertive Training for Women: A Report of a Questionnaire Study" (in preparation, 1975).

Notes

1. In a study done with three groups of mental health workers, one group was asked to describe a mature, healthy, socially competent adult man; another group was asked to characterize a mature, healthy, socially competent woman, and the third group was asked to identify a mature, healthy, socially competent adult person. Groups 1 and 2, respectively, defined a man as independent, aggressive, creative, and very active; and a woman as dependent, submissive, conscientious, and masochistic. The third group characterized a mature, healthy human being as independent, aggressive, creative, and active—the same as a healthy man. This implies a double standard of mental health and social behavior, from which one could infer that healthy women are not mature, socially competent human beings. Inge K. Broverman, Donald M. Broverman, Frank E. Clarkson, Paul S. Rosenkrantz, and Susan R. Vogel, "Sex-Role Stereotypes and Clinical Judgments of Mental Health," *Journal of Consulting and Clinical Psychology*, 1970, 34(1):1–7.

2. This biography has been adapted, in part, from an unpublished talk by Beverly Hotchner, Ph.D.

3. Arnold M. Lazarus, "Women in Behavior Therapy," *Women in Therapy: New Psychotherapies for a Changing Society*, ed. Violet Franks, Vasanti Burtle (New York: Brunner/Mazel, Inc., 1974), p. 218.

4. This chapter has relevance to Eric Berne's *Games People Play* (New York: Random House, 1964), though the material here is independent of Berne's book. Berne defines a "game" as "an ongoing series of complementary ulterior transactions progressing to a well-defined, predictable outcome." (p. 48) Unlike Berne, in this chapter we use the term "games" to refer to indirect, manipulative forms of non-assertive behavior, where the player tries to get what she wants without asking for it.

5. Marabel Morgan, *The Total Woman* (Old Tappan, N.J.: Fleming H. Revell Co., 1973), p. 71. See also p. 87.

6. Albert Ellis and R. A. Harper, *A Guide to Rational Living* (North Hollywood, Calif.: Wilshire Book Co., 1974), p. 79.

7. "The Instigations of Assertive Training," *Journal of Behavior Therapy and Experimental Psychiatry*, 1970, 1(2): 151.

8. Edmond Jacobson, *Progressive Relaxation* (Chicago: University of Chicago Press, 1938). Adaptation of his work.

9. Richard M. McFall and Diane B. Lillesand, "Behavior Rehearsal with Modeling and Coaching in Assertion Training," *Journal of Abnormal Psychology*, 1971, 3.

Black Tickets

Jayne Anne Phillips

"The unmistakable work of early genius."
—Tillie Olsen

Black Tickets is an astonishing collection of short stories that deals with the dreams and passions of young men and women and the desperate loneliness that pervades American life. It marks the debut of "the best short story writer since Eudora Welty."
—Nadine Gordimer

Laurel $3.95